50 Premium Mexican Cooking Recipes for Home

By: Kelly Johnson

Table of Contents

- Guacamole
- Tacos al Pastor
- Enchiladas Suizas
- Mole Poblano
- Carnitas
- Chiles Rellenos
- Pozole
- Sopa de Lima
- Cochinita Pibil
- Tamales
- Pico de Gallo
- Birria
- Quesadillas
- Fajitas
- Ceviche
- Huevos Rancheros
- Chilaquiles
- Tostadas
- Flan
- Churros
- Mexican Street Corn (Elote)
- Horchata
- Arroz con Leche
- Pollo con Mole Verde
- Chile Verde
- Camarones a la Diabla
- Barbacoa
- Papas con Chorizo
- Sopes
- Aguachile
- Caldo de Res
- Molletes
- Empanadas
- Camotes Enmielados
- Pescado a la Veracruzana
- Cochinita Pibil Tacos

- Tlacoyos
- Camarones al Mojo de Ajo
- Guajillo Chicken
- Pan de Elote
- Nopalitos Salad
- Jericalla
- Polvorones
- Huachinango a la Veracruzana
- Esquites
- Alambre
- Pescado Zarandeado
- Chile Ancho Rellenos
- Tacos de Cabeza
- Camotes Poblanos

Guacamole

Ingredients:

- 3 ripe avocados
- 1 lime, juiced
- 1/2 teaspoon salt (adjust to taste)
- 1/2 teaspoon ground cumin
- 1/2 teaspoon cayenne pepper (optional, for heat)
- 1/2 medium red onion, finely diced
- 2 small tomatoes, seeded and diced
- 2 tablespoons fresh cilantro, chopped
- 1 clove garlic, minced

Instructions:

1. Cut the avocados in half, remove the pits, and scoop the flesh into a mixing bowl.
2. Mash the avocados with a fork or potato masher until smooth or slightly chunky, depending on your preference.
3. Stir in the lime juice, salt, cumin, and cayenne pepper (if using), mixing well to combine.
4. Add the diced onion, tomatoes, cilantro, and minced garlic to the bowl. Gently fold the ingredients together until evenly distributed.
5. Taste and adjust seasoning if needed, adding more salt or lime juice according to your taste.
6. Serve immediately with tortilla chips or as a topping for tacos, nachos, or any Mexican dish.

Tips:

- To keep your guacamole from browning, press plastic wrap directly onto the surface of the guacamole to minimize contact with air, or store it in an airtight container.
- For extra flavor, you can add a pinch of smoked paprika or chopped jalapeño peppers to your guacamole.

Enjoy your homemade guacamole!

Tacos al Pastor

Ingredients:

For the Marinade:

- 3 dried guajillo chilies, stemmed and seeded
- 3 dried ancho chilies, stemmed and seeded
- 1/2 cup pineapple juice
- 1/4 cup orange juice
- 4 cloves garlic
- 1/2 small white onion, chopped
- 1 tablespoon achiote paste (optional, for color and flavor)
- 1 teaspoon dried oregano
- 1 teaspoon ground cumin
- 1 teaspoon ground coriander
- 1/2 teaspoon ground cinnamon
- 1/4 teaspoon ground cloves
- Salt and pepper, to taste

For the Tacos:

- 1 kg (about 2 lbs) pork shoulder, thinly sliced
- 1/2 pineapple, sliced into rounds
- Small corn tortillas
- Chopped cilantro, for garnish
- Diced white onion, for garnish
- Lime wedges, for serving

Instructions:

1. **Prepare the Marinade:**
    - In a bowl, pour hot water over the dried guajillo and ancho chilies. Let them soak for 15-20 minutes until softened.
    - Drain the chilies and transfer them to a blender.
    - Add pineapple juice, orange juice, garlic, chopped onion, achiote paste (if using), oregano, cumin, coriander, cinnamon, cloves, salt, and pepper to the blender.
    - Blend until smooth, adding a little water if needed to achieve a thick, pourable consistency.
2. **Marinate the Pork:**
    - Place the thinly sliced pork shoulder in a large bowl or resealable plastic bag.
    - Pour the marinade over the pork, making sure it's well coated. Cover (or seal the bag) and refrigerate for at least 2 hours, preferably overnight, to allow the flavors to develop.
3. **Cooking:**

- Preheat your grill or a large skillet over medium-high heat.
- Remove the marinated pork from the refrigerator and let it come to room temperature for about 20-30 minutes.
- If using a grill, skewer the marinated pork slices with pineapple rounds in between. Grill over medium-high heat, turning occasionally, until the pork is cooked through and slightly charred, about 8-10 minutes.
- If using a skillet, heat a bit of oil over medium-high heat. Cook the pork slices in batches until cooked through and slightly caramelized, about 5-7 minutes per batch.

4. **Assemble the Tacos:**
   - Warm the corn tortillas on a griddle or in a dry skillet until soft and pliable.
   - To assemble each taco, place a few slices of grilled pork with pineapple onto a warm tortilla.
   - Garnish with chopped cilantro, diced onion, and a squeeze of lime juice.
5. **Serve:**
   - Serve immediately with additional lime wedges and your favorite salsa or hot sauce on the side.

Enjoy your homemade Tacos al Pastor, a flavorful and satisfying Mexican dish!

Enchiladas Suizas

Ingredients:

For the Chicken:

- 2 boneless, skinless chicken breasts
- Water, for boiling
- Salt, to taste
- 1 bay leaf
- 1/4 onion, chopped

For the Green Sauce:

- 6 tomatillos, husked and rinsed
- 1 poblano pepper
- 1 jalapeño pepper (optional, for extra heat)
- 1/2 onion, chopped
- 2 cloves garlic, minced
- 1/2 cup chicken broth (reserved from cooking chicken)
- 1/2 cup sour cream
- 1/4 cup cilantro leaves
- Salt and pepper, to taste

For the Enchiladas:

- 12 corn tortillas
- Vegetable oil, for frying
- 1 cup shredded Monterey Jack cheese
- 1/2 cup crumbled queso fresco (optional, for garnish)
- Chopped cilantro, for garnish
- Sliced avocado, for serving

Instructions:

1. **Cook the Chicken:**
    - Place chicken breasts in a medium saucepan and cover with water.
    - Add salt, bay leaf, and chopped onion.
    - Bring to a boil over medium-high heat, then reduce heat to low and simmer until chicken is cooked through, about 15-20 minutes.
    - Remove chicken from broth, let cool slightly, and shred using two forks or your hands. Reserve 1/2 cup of the chicken broth for the sauce.
2. **Prepare the Green Sauce:**
    - In a dry skillet over medium-high heat, roast the tomatillos, poblano pepper, and jalapeño pepper until charred and softened, turning occasionally. This should take about 10 minutes.

- Transfer the roasted vegetables to a blender along with chopped onion, minced garlic, chicken broth, sour cream, cilantro leaves, salt, and pepper.
- Blend until smooth and creamy. Adjust seasoning to taste.

3. **Assemble the Enchiladas:**
   - Preheat your oven to 350°F (175°C).
   - Heat vegetable oil in a small skillet over medium heat. Lightly fry each tortilla for about 10-15 seconds per side until softened. Drain on paper towels.
   - Dip each tortilla into the green sauce to coat both sides.
   - Fill each tortilla with shredded chicken, roll up, and place seam-side down in a baking dish.
   - Pour remaining green sauce evenly over the enchiladas.
   - Sprinkle shredded Monterey Jack cheese on top.

4. **Bake:**
   - Cover the baking dish with foil and bake in the preheated oven for 20 minutes, or until the cheese is melted and the enchiladas are heated through.

5. **Serve:**
   - Remove from oven and sprinkle with crumbled queso fresco (if using) and chopped cilantro.
   - Serve hot, garnished with sliced avocado on the side.

Enjoy your homemade Enchiladas Suizas, creamy and full of flavor!

Mole Poblano

Ingredients:

For the Mole Sauce:

- 4 dried ancho chilies, stemmed and seeded
- 3 dried pasilla chilies, stemmed and seeded
- 2 dried mulato chilies, stemmed and seeded
- 1/2 cup raw almonds
- 1/4 cup raw peanuts
- 1/4 cup raisins
- 1/4 cup sesame seeds
- 1/4 cup pumpkin seeds (pepitas)
- 1/2 corn tortilla, torn into pieces
- 1 small onion, chopped
- 3 cloves garlic, minced
- 1/2 teaspoon ground cinnamon
- 1/2 teaspoon ground cloves
- 1/2 teaspoon ground coriander
- 1/2 teaspoon ground anise seeds (optional)
- 1/2 teaspoon dried thyme
- 1/2 teaspoon dried oregano
- 1/4 teaspoon ground black pepper
- 1/4 teaspoon ground cumin
- 4 cups chicken broth
- 1 tablet Mexican chocolate (such as Abuelita or Ibarra), chopped (about 3 ounces)
- Salt, to taste
- 2 tablespoons vegetable oil

For Serving:

- Cooked chicken or turkey, shredded or cut into pieces
- White rice, cooked

Instructions:

1. **Prepare the Chilies:**
    - Heat a dry skillet over medium-high heat. Toast the dried chilies for about 1-2 minutes per side until fragrant. Be careful not to burn them.
    - Transfer the toasted chilies to a bowl and cover with hot water. Let them soak for 20-30 minutes until softened.
2. **Toast and Prepare Ingredients:**

- In the same skillet, toast the almonds, peanuts, raisins, sesame seeds, pumpkin seeds, and torn tortilla piece until lightly browned and fragrant. Stir frequently to avoid burning.
- Remove from heat and set aside.

3. **Make the Mole Sauce:**
   - In a blender, combine the soaked chilies (discard soaking water), toasted nuts and seeds mixture, chopped onion, minced garlic, ground cinnamon, cloves, coriander, anise seeds (if using), thyme, oregano, black pepper, cumin, and 2 cups of chicken broth.
   - Blend until smooth, adding more chicken broth as needed to achieve a thick, pourable consistency.

4. **Cook the Mole:**
   - Heat vegetable oil in a large pot over medium heat.
   - Pour the blended mole sauce into the pot and cook, stirring constantly, for about 5 minutes to bring out the flavors.
   - Gradually add the remaining 2 cups of chicken broth, stirring to combine.
   - Add the chopped Mexican chocolate and continue stirring until melted and incorporated into the sauce.
   - Simmer the mole sauce over low heat for about 30-40 minutes, stirring occasionally, until it thickens and flavors meld together.
   - Taste and season with salt as needed.

5. **Serve:**
   - To serve, place cooked chicken or turkey pieces on a plate. Spoon the mole sauce generously over the meat.
   - Serve alongside white rice.

Enjoy your homemade Mole Poblano, a dish that showcases the richness and depth of Mexican culinary tradition!

Carnitas

Ingredients:

- 3-4 lbs pork shoulder (also known as pork butt), cut into 2-inch chunks
- 1 onion, quartered
- 4 cloves garlic, smashed
- 2 bay leaves
- 1 orange, juiced (about 1/2 cup)
- 1 lime, juiced (about 1/4 cup)
- 1/2 cup water or chicken broth
- 1 teaspoon ground cumin
- 1 teaspoon dried oregano
- 1 teaspoon chili powder
- 1 teaspoon paprika
- 1 teaspoon salt, plus more to taste
- Freshly ground black pepper, to taste
- Vegetable oil, for frying

Instructions:

1. **Prep the Pork:**
   - Trim excess fat from the pork shoulder and cut it into 2-inch chunks. Season generously with salt and pepper.
2. **Braise the Pork:**
   - In a large Dutch oven or heavy-bottomed pot, combine the pork chunks, quartered onion, smashed garlic cloves, bay leaves, orange juice, lime juice, water or chicken broth, ground cumin, dried oregano, chili powder, paprika, salt, and black pepper.
   - Bring the mixture to a boil over medium-high heat, then reduce the heat to low. Cover and simmer gently for about 2 to 2.5 hours, stirring occasionally, until the pork is very tender and can be easily shredded.
3. **Crisp the Carnitas:**
   - Preheat your oven broiler on high or a large skillet over medium-high heat.
   - Remove the pork pieces from the braising liquid and transfer them to a baking sheet lined with aluminum foil or a baking rack. Use a slotted spoon to avoid transferring too much liquid.
   - Shred the pork using two forks or tongs.
   - If using the oven broiler: Place the baking sheet under the broiler for about 5-7 minutes, until the edges of the pork start to crisp and brown. Watch closely to prevent burning.
   - If using a skillet: Heat a tablespoon of vegetable oil in the skillet over medium-high heat. Add the shredded pork in batches, pressing it down with a spatula to crisp up the edges. Cook for about 3-5 minutes per batch, turning occasionally, until crispy.

4. **Serve:**
    - Once crispy, remove the carnitas from the oven or skillet and transfer to a serving dish.
    - Serve the carnitas hot with warm tortillas and your favorite toppings such as diced onions, cilantro, salsa, guacamole, and lime wedges.

Enjoy your homemade Carnitas! They're perfect for tacos, burritos, nachos, or simply served with rice and beans.

Chiles Rellenos

Ingredients:

For the Filling:

- 4 large poblano peppers
- 1 cup shredded Oaxaca cheese or Monterey Jack cheese (for stuffing)
- Optional filling ideas: cooked shredded chicken, beef picadillo, or refried beans

For the Egg Batter:

- 4 large eggs, separated
- 1/4 teaspoon salt
- 1/4 teaspoon baking powder

For the Sauce (optional):

- 2 cups tomato sauce or salsa roja
- 1/2 onion, finely chopped
- 2 cloves garlic, minced
- 1 tablespoon vegetable oil
- Salt and pepper, to taste

For Frying:

- Vegetable oil, for frying

Instructions:

1. **Roast and Peel the Poblano Peppers:**
    - Preheat your broiler or grill to high heat.
    - Place the whole poblano peppers on a baking sheet or directly over the flame of the grill.
    - Roast the peppers, turning occasionally, until the skins are charred and blistered all over. This should take about 5-7 minutes in the broiler or 10-12 minutes on the grill.
    - Transfer the roasted peppers to a bowl and cover tightly with plastic wrap or a clean kitchen towel. Let them steam for about 10 minutes to loosen the skins.
    - Carefully peel off the charred skins from the peppers. Make a slit down the side of each pepper and remove the seeds and membranes, being careful not to tear the flesh.
2. **Prepare the Filling:**
    - Stuff each roasted poblano pepper with shredded cheese or your desired filling (such as cooked shredded chicken, beef picadillo, or refried beans). Be generous but ensure the peppers can still be closed.

3. **Prepare the Egg Batter:**
   - In a large bowl, beat the egg whites with an electric mixer until stiff peaks form.
   - In a separate bowl, whisk together the egg yolks, salt, and baking powder until smooth.
   - Gently fold the egg yolk mixture into the beaten egg whites until combined. This will create a light and fluffy batter.
4. **Coat and Fry the Chiles Rellenos:**
   - Heat about 1 inch of vegetable oil in a large skillet over medium-high heat until hot but not smoking.
   - Carefully dip each stuffed poblano pepper into the egg batter, coating it evenly on all sides.
   - Using tongs, carefully place the coated pepper into the hot oil. Fry until golden and crispy on one side, about 2-3 minutes, then carefully flip and fry the other side until golden brown and crispy.
   - Remove the fried chile relleno from the oil and place on a plate lined with paper towels to drain excess oil. Repeat with the remaining stuffed peppers.
5. **Make the Sauce (optional):**
   - In a saucepan, heat vegetable oil over medium heat. Add finely chopped onion and minced garlic, and sauté until softened and fragrant, about 3-4 minutes.
   - Add tomato sauce or salsa roja to the pan. Season with salt and pepper to taste. Simmer for 5-7 minutes, stirring occasionally, until heated through.
6. **Serve:**
   - Place each fried chile relleno on a plate and spoon the optional sauce over the top.
   - Serve hot, garnished with additional cheese, cilantro, and sour cream if desired.

Enjoy your homemade Chiles Rellenos, a delicious and satisfying dish that showcases the flavors of Mexico!

Pozole

Ingredients:

For the Pozole:

- 2 lbs pork shoulder, cut into chunks
- 1 onion, peeled and halved
- 4 cloves garlic, peeled
- 2 bay leaves
- Salt, to taste
- 1 tbsp vegetable oil
- 1 can (29 oz) hominy, drained and rinsed (or 2 cups dried hominy, soaked overnight and cooked until tender)
- 6 cups chicken broth

For the Red Chili Sauce:

- 3 dried guajillo chilies, stemmed and seeded
- 2 dried pasilla chilies, stemmed and seeded
- 2 dried ancho chilies, stemmed and seeded
- 4 cups water, divided
- 1/2 onion, chopped
- 3 cloves garlic, minced
- 1 tsp dried oregano
- 1/2 tsp ground cumin
- 1/2 tsp ground coriander
- Salt, to taste

For Serving (optional):

- Shredded cabbage or lettuce
- Sliced radishes
- Chopped cilantro
- Lime wedges
- Sliced avocado
- Tostadas or tortilla chips

Instructions:

1. **Prepare the Pork:**
    - In a large pot, add the pork shoulder chunks, halved onion, peeled garlic cloves, bay leaves, and a pinch of salt.
    - Cover with water and bring to a boil over high heat. Reduce heat to medium-low and simmer for about 1.5 to 2 hours, until the pork is tender and cooked through. Skim off any foam or impurities that rise to the surface.

2. **Make the Red Chili Sauce:**
    - While the pork is cooking, prepare the red chili sauce. In a dry skillet over medium-high heat, toast the dried guajillo, pasilla, and ancho chilies for about 30 seconds per side until fragrant. Be careful not to burn them.
    - Transfer the toasted chilies to a saucepan and cover with 3 cups of water. Bring to a boil, then reduce heat and simmer for about 15 minutes until the chilies are softened.
    - Using a slotted spoon, transfer the softened chilies to a blender. Add the chopped onion, minced garlic, dried oregano, ground cumin, ground coriander, and a pinch of salt.
    - Strain the soaking liquid from the chilies and add 1 cup of it to the blender (discard the remaining liquid). Blend until smooth, adding more water if needed to achieve a pourable sauce consistency. Set aside.
3. **Prepare the Hominy:**
    - If using dried hominy, soak it overnight in water, then cook until tender according to package instructions. Drain and set aside.
4. **Finish the Pozole:**
    - Once the pork is tender, remove it from the broth and shred it using two forks.
    - In the same pot with the pork broth, heat vegetable oil over medium heat. Add the red chili sauce and stir well to combine. Simmer for about 10 minutes to allow the flavors to meld.
    - Add the drained and rinsed hominy to the pot along with the shredded pork. Stir to combine.
    - Add chicken broth gradually, stirring until you reach your desired consistency. Pozole should be soupy but hearty.
    - Season with salt to taste and simmer for another 15-20 minutes to heat everything through.
5. **Serve:**
    - Ladle the pozole into bowls. Serve hot with shredded cabbage or lettuce, sliced radishes, chopped cilantro, lime wedges, sliced avocado, and tostadas or tortilla chips on the side.
    - Let each person customize their pozole with their preferred toppings.

Enjoy your homemade Pozole Rojo, a comforting and flavorful Mexican soup!

Sopa de Lima

Ingredients:

For the Soup:

- 2 boneless, skinless chicken breasts
- 6 cups chicken broth
- 1 onion, chopped
- 2 cloves garlic, minced
- 2 tomatoes, diced
- 1 green bell pepper, diced
- 1 red bell pepper, diced
- 2 stalks celery, diced
- 2 carrots, diced
- 2 bay leaves
- 1 teaspoon dried oregano
- 1 teaspoon ground cumin
- 1 teaspoon ground coriander
- Salt and pepper, to taste
- 1/4 cup fresh cilantro, chopped
- Juice of 2-3 limes (adjust to taste)

For Garnish:

- Tortilla chips or strips
- Avocado, diced
- Fresh cilantro, chopped
- Sliced jalapeños (optional)
- Lime wedges

Instructions:

1. **Cook the Chicken:**
    - In a large pot, bring the chicken broth to a boil over medium-high heat.
    - Add the chicken breasts, reduce heat to medium-low, and simmer for about 15-20 minutes, until the chicken is cooked through.
    - Remove the chicken from the broth and shred it using two forks. Set aside.
2. **Prepare the Soup Base:**
    - In the same pot with the chicken broth, add chopped onion, minced garlic, diced tomatoes, diced green and red bell peppers, diced celery, diced carrots, bay leaves, dried oregano, ground cumin, ground coriander, salt, and pepper.
    - Simmer over medium heat for about 15-20 minutes, until the vegetables are tender and the flavors have melded.
3. **Add the Shredded Chicken and Lime Juice:**

- Return the shredded chicken to the pot.
- Stir in the chopped cilantro and lime juice. Adjust the amount of lime juice to your taste preference, balancing the tanginess with the other flavors.
4. **Serve:**
    - Ladle the Sopa de Lima into bowls.
    - Serve hot, garnished with tortilla chips or strips, diced avocado, chopped cilantro, sliced jalapeños (if using), and lime wedges on the side.

Enjoy your homemade Sopa de Lima, a comforting and flavorful soup that's perfect for any occasion!

Cochinita Pibil

Ingredients:

For the Marinade:

- 3-4 lbs pork shoulder or pork butt, cut into chunks
- 1 cup orange juice (about 3-4 oranges)
- 1/2 cup lime juice (about 4-5 limes)
- 1/2 cup achiote paste
- 4 cloves garlic, minced
- 1 tbsp dried oregano
- 1 tbsp ground cumin
- 1 tbsp ground coriander
- 1 tsp ground cloves
- 1 tsp ground cinnamon
- Salt, to taste
- Black pepper, to taste

For Cooking:

- Banana leaves (optional, for wrapping and serving)
- 1 onion, thinly sliced
- 1-2 habanero or jalapeño peppers, thinly sliced (optional, for heat)
- Vegetable oil, for cooking

For Serving:

- Corn tortillas
- Pickled red onions (optional)
- Fresh cilantro, chopped
- Lime wedges

Instructions:

1. **Prepare the Marinade:**
    - In a blender or food processor, combine orange juice, lime juice, achiote paste, minced garlic, dried oregano, ground cumin, ground coriander, ground cloves, ground cinnamon, salt, and black pepper. Blend until smooth.
2. **Marinate the Pork:**
    - Place the pork chunks in a large bowl or resealable plastic bag.
    - Pour the marinade over the pork, making sure each piece is well coated. Cover (or seal the bag) and refrigerate for at least 4 hours, preferably overnight, to allow the flavors to penetrate the meat.
3. **Cooking Cochinita Pibil:**
    - Preheat your oven to 325°F (160°C).

- If using banana leaves, briefly pass them over an open flame to soften and make them pliable. Line a baking dish with banana leaves, letting them hang over the edges (if available). If not using banana leaves, you can still cook the pork directly in a baking dish.
- Place the marinated pork and marinade into the lined baking dish. Spread the thinly sliced onion and sliced peppers (if using) over the top.
- Cover tightly with more banana leaves or aluminum foil to seal in the juices.
- Bake in the preheated oven for about 3-4 hours, until the pork is very tender and easily pulls apart with a fork.

4. **Serve Cochinita Pibil:**
   - Once cooked, remove the baking dish from the oven and let it rest for a few minutes.
   - Shred the pork using two forks directly in the baking dish, mixing it with the juices and onions.
   - Serve Cochinita Pibil hot, wrapped in warm corn tortillas.
   - Garnish with pickled red onions (if using), chopped cilantro, and a squeeze of fresh lime juice.

Enjoy your homemade Cochinita Pibil, a delicious and aromatic dish that captures the flavors of Yucatán cuisine!

Tamales

Ingredients:

For the Pork Filling:

- 1 lb pork shoulder or pork butt, cut into chunks
- 1 onion, chopped
- 2 cloves garlic, minced
- 1 tsp ground cumin
- 1 tsp dried oregano
- 1/2 tsp ground coriander
- Salt and pepper, to taste
- Water or chicken broth, as needed

For the Masa Dough:

- 2 cups masa harina (corn flour for tamales)
- 1 cup chicken broth, warmed
- 1/2 cup lard or vegetable shortening
- 1 tsp baking powder
- 1/2 tsp salt
- Corn husks, soaked in warm water for 30 minutes and drained

Instructions:

1. **Prepare the Pork Filling:**
   - In a large pot or Dutch oven, combine the pork chunks, chopped onion, minced garlic, ground cumin, dried oregano, ground coriander, salt, and pepper.
   - Add enough water or chicken broth to cover the pork.
   - Bring to a boil over medium-high heat, then reduce the heat to low. Cover and simmer for about 1.5 to 2 hours, until the pork is tender and can be easily shredded.
   - Remove the pork from the pot and shred it using two forks. Set aside.
2. **Prepare the Masa Dough:**
   - In a large mixing bowl, combine the masa harina, warm chicken broth, lard or vegetable shortening, baking powder, and salt.
   - Mix with your hands or a spoon until well combined and the dough is smooth and slightly sticky. The consistency should be like soft cookie dough. If needed, add more broth or water, a few tablespoons at a time.
3. **Assemble the Tamales:**
   - Take a soaked corn husk and pat it dry with a clean towel.
   - Spread about 2 tablespoons of the masa dough evenly onto the center of the husk, leaving a border along the edges.
   - Place a spoonful of the shredded pork filling in the center of the masa.

- Fold one side of the husk over the filling, then fold the other side to cover.
- Fold up the bottom (narrow end) of the husk.
- Place the tamale seam-side down on a tray, and repeat with the remaining husks, masa dough, and filling.

4. **Steam the Tamales:**
    - Fill the bottom of a large steamer pot with water, making sure the water level is below the steamer basket or rack.
    - Stand the tamales upright in the steamer basket, open end up, with the folded end facing down.
    - Cover the tamales with a layer of leftover corn husks or a clean kitchen towel.
    - Cover the pot with a lid and steam over medium heat for about 1.5 to 2 hours, or until the masa is firm and easily pulls away from the husk.

5. **Serve:**
    - Let the tamales rest for a few minutes before serving.
    - Unwrap the tamales and serve warm.
    - Enjoy your delicious homemade pork tamales with salsa, sour cream, or your favorite toppings.

Tamales are a labor of love but are well worth the effort for their delicious flavors and cultural significance. Adjust fillings and seasonings to suit your taste preferences, and enjoy this authentic Mexican dish!

Pico de Gallo

Ingredients:

- 4 medium ripe tomatoes, diced
- 1/2 cup finely chopped white onion
- 1/2 cup chopped fresh cilantro
- 1-2 jalapeño or serrano peppers, seeded and finely chopped (adjust to your spice preference)
- Juice of 1-2 limes
- Salt, to taste

Instructions:

1. **Prepare the Ingredients:**
    - Dice the tomatoes, finely chop the onion, cilantro, and peppers. Remove the seeds from the peppers if you prefer a milder salsa.
2. **Combine Ingredients:**
    - In a mixing bowl, combine the diced tomatoes, chopped onion, chopped cilantro, and chopped peppers.
3. **Season:**
    - Squeeze fresh lime juice over the mixture. Start with the juice of one lime and add more to taste.
    - Season with salt to taste. Mix well to combine all the ingredients evenly.
4. **Chill (optional):**
    - For best flavor, let the Pico de Gallo sit in the refrigerator for about 30 minutes to allow the flavors to meld together. This step is optional but recommended.
5. **Serve:**
    - Serve Pico de Gallo fresh as a topping or side dish for tacos, burritos, nachos, grilled meats, or alongside tortilla chips.
    - Store any leftovers in an airtight container in the refrigerator for up to 2-3 days.

Pico de Gallo is a simple and delicious way to enjoy the flavors of fresh ingredients and adds a zesty kick to your favorite Mexican-inspired dishes. Adjust the spiciness by adding more or less jalapeño or serrano peppers according to your taste preference. Enjoy!

Birria

Ingredients:

For the Birria:

- 3 lbs beef chuck roast or brisket, cut into chunks
- 3 dried guajillo chilies, stemmed and seeded
- 3 dried ancho chilies, stemmed and seeded
- 1 onion, quartered
- 5 cloves garlic, peeled
- 1 inch piece of ginger, peeled
- 1 cinnamon stick
- 4 cloves
- 1 tsp dried oregano
- 1 tsp ground cumin
- 1 tsp ground coriander
- 1/2 tsp ground black pepper
- Salt, to taste
- 2 cups beef broth
- 2 tbsp vegetable oil

For Serving:

- Corn tortillas
- Chopped fresh cilantro
- Diced onion
- Lime wedges
- Salsa or hot sauce of choice

Instructions:

1. **Prepare the Chilies:**
    - Heat a dry skillet over medium heat and toast the dried guajillo and ancho chilies for about 1-2 minutes per side until fragrant and slightly puffed. Be careful not to burn them.
    - Transfer the toasted chilies to a bowl and cover with hot water. Let them soak for about 20 minutes until softened.
2. **Make the Birria Paste:**
    - In a blender or food processor, combine the soaked chilies (discarding the soaking water), quartered onion, garlic cloves, peeled ginger, cinnamon stick, cloves, dried oregano, ground cumin, ground coriander, black pepper, and salt to taste.
    - Blend until smooth, adding a little beef broth if needed to achieve a thick paste consistency.

3. **Cook the Birria:**
    - In a large pot or Dutch oven, heat vegetable oil over medium-high heat.
    - Add the beef chunks in batches and sear them until browned on all sides. Remove and set aside.
    - In the same pot, add the birria paste and cook over medium heat for about 5 minutes, stirring constantly, until fragrant.
    - Return the seared beef chunks to the pot. Add the remaining beef broth and stir to combine.
    - Bring the mixture to a boil, then reduce the heat to low. Cover and simmer for about 2.5 to 3 hours, or until the beef is very tender and falls apart easily when shredded with a fork.
    - Stir occasionally and add more water or broth if needed to keep the meat covered.
4. **Serve Birria:**
    - Once the birria is cooked and tender, remove the cinnamon stick.
    - Serve the birria hot in bowls, garnished with chopped fresh cilantro and diced onion.
    - Serve with warm corn tortillas on the side, lime wedges, and salsa or hot sauce for dipping or drizzling.
5. **Enjoy:**
    - Dip the tortillas into the flavorful broth (consommé) and fill them with the tender birria meat, cilantro, onion, and a squeeze of lime juice.
    - Enjoy your homemade Birria de Res, a delicious and comforting Mexican dish!

Birria is perfect for sharing with family and friends, especially during special occasions or gatherings. Adjust the spiciness and seasoning to your preference and savor the rich flavors of this traditional Mexican recipe.

Quesadillas

Ingredients:

- 4 large flour tortillas (you can also use corn tortillas if preferred)
- 2 cups shredded cheese (such as Monterey Jack, Cheddar, or a Mexican blend)
- Optional fillings: cooked chicken, beef, shrimp, beans, sautéed vegetables, sliced jalapeños, etc.
- Optional toppings: salsa, guacamole, sour cream, chopped cilantro, diced tomatoes, etc.
- Cooking oil or butter, for cooking

Instructions:

1. **Prepare the Fillings (if using):**
   - If adding any fillings like cooked chicken, beef, shrimp, or sautéed vegetables, make sure they are cooked and ready to use.
2. **Assemble the Quesadillas:**
   - Heat a large skillet or griddle over medium heat.
   - Place one tortilla flat on the skillet.
   - Sprinkle about 1/2 cup of shredded cheese evenly over the tortilla.
   - Add any desired fillings over half of the tortilla (if using).
   - Fold the tortilla in half over the cheese and fillings, pressing down gently with a spatula.
3. **Cook the Quesadilla:**
   - Cook the quesadilla for about 2-3 minutes on each side, or until the tortilla is golden brown and crispy, and the cheese is melted.
   - If needed, you can add a small amount of oil or butter to the skillet before flipping to help crisp up the tortilla.
4. **Repeat for Remaining Quesadillas:**
   - Remove the cooked quesadilla from the skillet and place it on a cutting board.
   - Cut into wedges using a sharp knife or pizza cutter.
   - Repeat the process with the remaining tortillas and fillings.
5. **Serve:**
   - Serve the quesadilla wedges hot, garnished with your favorite toppings such as salsa, guacamole, sour cream, chopped cilantro, or diced tomatoes.

Variations:

- **Chicken or Beef Quesadillas:** Add cooked and shredded chicken or beef along with cheese for a heartier quesadilla.
- **Vegetarian Quesadillas:** Fill with sautéed vegetables like bell peppers, onions, and mushrooms.
- **Seafood Quesadillas:** Use cooked shrimp or fish as a filling option.
- **Breakfast Quesadillas:** Fill with scrambled eggs, cheese, and your choice of breakfast meats like bacon or sausage.

- **Spicy Quesadillas:** Add sliced jalapeños or chipotle peppers for a kick of heat.

Quesadillas are versatile and easy to customize with your favorite ingredients. They make a quick and satisfying meal or snack, perfect for any time of day. Enjoy experimenting with different fillings and toppings to create your own delicious quesadilla variations!

Fajitas

Ingredients:

For the Chicken Marinade:

- 1 lb boneless, skinless chicken breasts or thighs, sliced into thin strips
- Juice of 1 lime
- 2 tbsp olive oil
- 2 cloves garlic, minced
- 1 tsp ground cumin
- 1 tsp chili powder
- 1/2 tsp paprika
- 1/2 tsp dried oregano
- Salt and pepper, to taste

For the Fajitas:

- 2 bell peppers (1 red, 1 green), thinly sliced
- 1 onion, thinly sliced
- 2 tbsp vegetable oil or olive oil
- Salt and pepper, to taste
- 8-10 small flour tortillas (or corn tortillas for a gluten-free option)
- Optional toppings: shredded cheese, guacamole, salsa, sour cream, chopped cilantro, lime wedges

Instructions:

1. **Marinate the Chicken:**
    - In a bowl or resealable plastic bag, combine the sliced chicken with lime juice, olive oil, minced garlic, ground cumin, chili powder, paprika, dried oregano, salt, and pepper.
    - Mix well to coat the chicken evenly. Marinate for at least 30 minutes, or up to 2 hours in the refrigerator.
2. **Prepare the Vegetables:**
    - While the chicken is marinating, slice the bell peppers and onion into thin strips.
3. **Cook the Fajitas:**
    - Heat 1 tablespoon of vegetable oil in a large skillet or cast iron pan over medium-high heat.
    - Add the sliced bell peppers and onion to the skillet. Season with salt and pepper. Cook, stirring occasionally, for about 5-7 minutes until the vegetables are tender and slightly charred. Remove from the skillet and set aside.
4. **Cook the Chicken:**
    - In the same skillet, heat the remaining tablespoon of oil over medium-high heat.

- Add the marinated chicken strips in a single layer, allowing them to cook undisturbed for 2-3 minutes to get a nice sear.
- Stir and cook for another 4-5 minutes, or until the chicken is cooked through and no longer pink inside.

5. **Assemble the Fajitas:**
    - Warm the tortillas in a dry skillet or wrap them in foil and heat in the oven until warmed through.
    - Serve the cooked chicken and sautéed vegetables on a platter.
    - Let everyone assemble their own fajitas by placing some chicken and vegetables in a tortilla.
    - Add optional toppings such as shredded cheese, guacamole, salsa, sour cream, chopped cilantro, and a squeeze of lime juice.
6. **Serve:**
    - Roll up the tortillas and enjoy your delicious homemade chicken fajitas!

Fajitas are versatile, so feel free to customize them with your favorite meats or seafood, and adjust the seasonings and toppings to your taste. They make for a fun and interactive meal that's perfect for family dinners or gatherings with friends.

Ceviche

Ingredients:

- 1 lb fresh white fish fillets (such as tilapia, sea bass, or halibut), cut into small bite-sized pieces
- 1 cup freshly squeezed lime juice (about 8-10 limes)
- 1 small red onion, thinly sliced
- 1-2 fresh jalapeño peppers, seeded and finely chopped (adjust to taste)
- 1-2 tomatoes, diced
- 1/2 cup chopped fresh cilantro
- Salt and pepper, to taste
- Optional: 1 avocado, diced (for serving)
- Optional: Tortilla chips or toasted corn nuts (for serving)

Instructions:

1. **Prepare the Fish:**
    - Cut the fish fillets into small bite-sized pieces and place them in a non-reactive (glass or ceramic) bowl.
2. **Marinate the Fish:**
    - Pour the freshly squeezed lime juice over the fish pieces, ensuring they are fully submerged. The lime juice should cover the fish completely to ensure even "cooking". Stir gently to coat.
    - Cover the bowl with plastic wrap and refrigerate for about 30 minutes to 1 hour. During this time, the fish will turn opaque and "cook" in the citrus juice.
3. **Prepare the Vegetables:**
    - Meanwhile, prepare the other ingredients. Thinly slice the red onion, chop the jalapeño peppers (adjust the amount to your desired level of spiciness), dice the tomatoes, and chop the fresh cilantro.
4. **Combine Ingredients:**
    - After marinating, drain most of the lime juice from the fish. You can leave a little juice to keep the ceviche moist.
    - Add the sliced red onion, chopped jalapeño peppers, diced tomatoes, and chopped cilantro to the fish. Season with salt and pepper to taste.
    - Gently toss the ingredients together until well combined.
5. **Chill and Serve:**
    - Cover the ceviche and refrigerate for another 15-30 minutes to allow the flavors to meld together.
    - Just before serving, taste and adjust seasoning if needed.
    - Optionally, add diced avocado for extra creaminess and texture.
    - Serve the ceviche cold, either in small bowls or martini glasses, garnished with additional cilantro leaves and accompanied by tortilla chips or toasted corn nuts.

Ceviche is best enjoyed fresh and chilled, making it a perfect appetizer or light meal on a hot day. It's important to use fresh and high-quality seafood for ceviche, and ensure it is properly marinated in citrus juice to achieve the desired texture and flavor. Adjust the amount of lime juice and spiciness according to your preference for a personalized ceviche experience!

Huevos Rancheros

Ingredients:

For the Ranchero Sauce:

- 2 tbsp vegetable oil
- 1 onion, finely chopped
- 2 cloves garlic, minced
- 1 jalapeño or serrano pepper, seeded and minced (optional, for heat)
- 1 can (14 oz) diced tomatoes (or 2 cups fresh diced tomatoes)
- 1 tsp ground cumin
- 1 tsp chili powder
- Salt and pepper, to taste

For the Huevos Rancheros:

- 4 corn tortillas
- 4 large eggs
- 1 tbsp vegetable oil
- Salt and pepper, to taste
- Optional toppings: chopped cilantro, sliced avocado, crumbled queso fresco or shredded cheese, sour cream, lime wedges

Instructions:

1. **Prepare the Ranchero Sauce:**
    - Heat vegetable oil in a skillet over medium heat.
    - Add finely chopped onion and cook until softened and translucent, about 5 minutes.
    - Stir in minced garlic and jalapeño or serrano pepper (if using), and cook for 1-2 minutes until fragrant.
    - Add diced tomatoes (with their juices), ground cumin, chili powder, salt, and pepper. Stir well to combine.
    - Bring the sauce to a simmer, then reduce the heat to low. Cook uncovered for about 10-15 minutes, stirring occasionally, until the sauce has thickened slightly.
2. **Prepare the Tortillas:**
    - In a separate skillet, heat 1 tablespoon of vegetable oil over medium heat.
    - Lightly fry each corn tortilla for about 1-2 minutes on each side until lightly golden and crispy. Drain on paper towels to remove excess oil.
3. **Cook the Eggs:**
    - In the same skillet used for frying the tortillas, add a little more oil if needed.
    - Crack the eggs into the skillet, leaving space between each egg.
    - Season with salt and pepper to taste. Cook the eggs to your desired doneness (typically sunny-side-up or over-easy).

4. **Assemble Huevos Rancheros:**
    - Place a fried tortilla on a serving plate.
    - Spoon a generous amount of the Ranchero sauce over the tortilla.
    - Carefully place a cooked egg on top of the sauce.
    - Repeat with the remaining tortillas, sauce, and eggs.
5. **Serve:**
    - Garnish the Huevos Rancheros with optional toppings such as chopped cilantro, sliced avocado, crumbled queso fresco or shredded cheese, sour cream, and lime wedges.
    - Serve immediately, with warm corn tortillas on the side if desired.

Enjoy your homemade Huevos Rancheros, a delicious and satisfying breakfast that showcases the vibrant flavors of Mexican cuisine! Adjust the spiciness of the Ranchero sauce by adding more or less chili according to your taste preferences.

Chilaquiles

Ingredients:

- 12 corn tortillas, preferably a day old (or you can use store-bought tortilla chips)
- 1 cup green salsa (salsa verde) - you can make your own or use store-bought
- 1 cup chicken broth (vegetable broth for vegetarian option)
- 1/2 cup chopped white onion
- 1/4 cup chopped cilantro
- 1 cup shredded chicken (optional)
- 1/2 cup crumbled queso fresco or shredded Mexican cheese blend
- 1/4 cup Mexican crema or sour cream
- 2 tablespoons vegetable oil
- Salt, to taste
- Optional toppings: sliced avocado, radishes, chopped cilantro, lime wedges

Instructions:

1. **Prepare Tortilla Strips:**
   - If using fresh tortillas, cut them into triangles or strips. If using day-old tortillas, cut them first, then let them sit out to dry a bit if they're not already crispy.
2. **Fry Tortilla Strips:**
   - Heat the vegetable oil in a large skillet over medium-high heat. Fry the tortilla strips in batches until golden and crispy. Remove to a paper towel-lined plate to drain excess oil. Season lightly with salt while still warm.
3. **Make the Sauce:**
   - In the same skillet, add the chopped onion and cook until softened, about 2-3 minutes.
   - Add the green salsa and chicken broth to the skillet. Bring to a simmer and let cook for about 5 minutes until slightly thickened.
4. **Simmer Tortilla Strips:**
   - Add the fried tortilla strips to the skillet with the green salsa mixture. Gently toss to coat the tortilla strips evenly. If using shredded chicken, add it now and stir to combine. Cook for another 2-3 minutes until the tortilla strips have softened slightly but are still holding their shape.
5. **Serve:**
   - Transfer the chilaquiles to serving plates or a platter. Sprinkle with crumbled queso fresco (or shredded cheese blend), chopped cilantro, and drizzle with Mexican crema (or sour cream).
6. **Add Toppings:**
   - Garnish with optional toppings such as sliced avocado, radishes, more chopped cilantro, and lime wedges.
7. **Enjoy:**

- Serve immediately while still hot and crispy. Chilaquiles are often enjoyed for breakfast or brunch but are delicious any time of day!

This recipe is versatile, so feel free to adjust the toppings and spice level according to your preference. It's a comforting and flavorful dish that's sure to be a hit!

Tostadas

Ingredients:

- 6 corn tortillas
- 1 cup cooked and shredded chicken (seasoned with salt and pepper)
- 1 cup refried beans (homemade or canned)
- 1 cup shredded lettuce
- 1/2 cup diced tomatoes
- 1/2 cup shredded cheese (such as Monterey Jack or Cheddar)
- 1/4 cup diced red onion
- 1/4 cup chopped cilantro
- 1 avocado, sliced
- Sour cream or Mexican crema, for topping
- Salsa or hot sauce, for topping
- Vegetable oil, for frying tortillas
- Salt and pepper, to taste

Instructions:

1. **Prepare the Tostada Shells:**
   - In a large skillet, heat about 1/4 inch of vegetable oil over medium-high heat.
   - Fry the corn tortillas one at a time in the hot oil, flipping once, until golden and crispy, about 1-2 minutes per side. Drain on paper towels and sprinkle lightly with salt. Alternatively, you can bake the tortillas in the oven until crispy.
2. **Assemble the Tostadas:**
   - Spread a layer of refried beans onto each crispy tortilla shell.
   - Top with shredded chicken, shredded lettuce, diced tomatoes, shredded cheese, diced red onion, chopped cilantro, and sliced avocado.
3. **Add Toppings:**
   - Drizzle with sour cream or Mexican crema.
   - Add salsa or hot sauce according to your preference for spiciness.
4. **Serve:**
   - Serve immediately while the tortillas are still crispy.

Tips:

- **Variations:** You can customize your tostadas with different toppings such as guacamole, pickled jalapeños, black beans, grilled vegetables, or even seafood like shrimp or fish.
- **Preparation:** If you prefer, you can use store-bought tostada shells instead of frying your own tortillas.
- **Make it Vegan:** Omit the chicken and cheese, and use vegan refried beans and vegan sour cream for a delicious vegan version.

Tostadas are versatile and can be served as a main dish or as part of a larger meal. They're perfect for gatherings or as a quick and satisfying dinner option. Enjoy your homemade tostadas!

Flan

Ingredients:

For the caramel:

- 1 cup granulated sugar
- 1/4 cup water

For the flan:

- 4 large eggs
- 1 can (14 oz) sweetened condensed milk
- 1 can (12 oz) evaporated milk
- 1 teaspoon vanilla extract
- Pinch of salt

Instructions:

1. **Prepare the Caramel:**
   - In a heavy-bottomed saucepan, combine the sugar and water over medium-high heat. Stir until the sugar dissolves.
   - Stop stirring and let the mixture come to a boil. Swirl the pan occasionally to ensure even caramelization. Cook until the caramel turns a golden amber color, about 5-7 minutes.
   - Immediately pour the caramel into a 9-inch round baking dish or several smaller ramekins, swirling to coat the bottom evenly. Be careful as the caramel is extremely hot. Set aside to cool and harden.
2. **Preheat the Oven:**
   - Preheat your oven to 350°F (175°C).
3. **Prepare the Flan Mixture:**
   - In a large bowl, whisk the eggs until well beaten.
   - Add the sweetened condensed milk, evaporated milk, vanilla extract, and a pinch of salt. Whisk until everything is thoroughly combined and smooth.
4. **Assemble and Bake:**
   - Pour the flan mixture gently over the hardened caramel in the baking dish or ramekins.
   - Place the baking dish or ramekins into a larger baking pan. Fill the larger pan with hot water until it reaches halfway up the sides of the flan dish(es). This water bath (bain-marie) will help the flan cook gently and evenly.
5. **Bake the Flan:**
   - Carefully transfer the pan to the preheated oven.
   - Bake for 50-60 minutes (for a large flan dish) or 30-40 minutes (for smaller ramekins), or until the flan is set but still slightly jiggly in the center.
6. **Cool and Chill:**

- Remove the flan from the water bath and let it cool to room temperature.
- Once cooled, cover and refrigerate for at least 4 hours, preferably overnight, to allow the flavors to meld and the flan to fully set.

7. **Serve:**
   - To serve, run a knife around the edge of the flan to loosen it from the dish.
   - Place a serving plate upside down over the baking dish or ramekin, then quickly and carefully invert it. The caramel will flow over the flan, creating a beautiful topping.

8. **Enjoy:**
   - Slice and serve the flan chilled. It's wonderfully creamy with a rich caramel flavor and makes for an elegant and satisfying dessert.

Tips:

- **Avoid Overmixing:** When whisking the flan mixture, avoid vigorous mixing to prevent incorporating too much air, which can create bubbles in the flan.
- **Storage:** Flan can be stored covered in the refrigerator for up to 3-4 days.
- **Variations:** You can infuse the milk with cinnamon sticks or citrus zest for additional flavor variations.

Flan is a timeless dessert that's perfect for any occasion, from casual dinners to special celebrations. Enjoy making and savoring this classic treat!

Churros

Ingredients:

- 1 cup water
- 1/2 cup unsalted butter
- 1 tablespoon granulated sugar
- 1/4 teaspoon salt
- 1 cup all-purpose flour
- 2 large eggs
- Vegetable oil, for frying
- 1/2 cup granulated sugar (for coating)
- 1 teaspoon ground cinnamon (for coating)
- Chocolate sauce or dulce de leche, for dipping (optional)

Instructions:

1. **Prepare the Dough:**
    - In a medium saucepan, combine water, butter, sugar, and salt. Bring to a boil over medium-high heat.
    - Reduce the heat to low and add the flour all at once. Stir vigorously with a wooden spoon until the mixture forms a ball and pulls away from the sides of the pan. This should take about 1-2 minutes.
    - Remove the pan from heat and let the dough cool for 5-10 minutes.
2. **Add Eggs:**
    - Add the eggs, one at a time, stirring well after each addition until fully incorporated. The dough should become smooth and shiny.
3. **Heat Oil:**
    - In a large, deep skillet or pot, heat about 2 inches of vegetable oil over medium-high heat until it reaches 350°F (175°C). Use a candy thermometer to monitor the temperature.
4. **Pipe Churros:**
    - Transfer the churro dough to a piping bag fitted with a large star tip (such as Wilton 1M). Alternatively, you can use a sturdy plastic bag with a corner snipped off.
    - Pipe 4-6 inch strips of dough directly into the hot oil, using kitchen scissors to cut the dough from the piping tip. Fry 3-4 churros at a time, depending on the size of your pan, to avoid overcrowding.
5. **Fry Churros:**
    - Fry the churros for about 2-3 minutes per side, or until they are golden brown and crispy. Use tongs to turn them as needed.
6. **Coat Churros:**

- In a shallow dish, mix together the granulated sugar and ground cinnamon. While the churros are still warm, roll them in the cinnamon sugar mixture until evenly coated.
7. **Serve:**
    - Serve the churros warm, optionally with chocolate sauce or dulce de leche for dipping.

Tips:

- **Piping Tips:** If you don't have a star tip, you can simply cut the dough into strips with a knife. The star tip creates the classic ridged texture on the churros.
- **Oil Temperature:** Maintain the oil temperature around 350°F (175°C) throughout frying to ensure crispy churros.
- **Dipping Sauces:** Churros are traditionally served with chocolate sauce, but you can also try caramel sauce, dulce de leche, or even fruit preserves.

Enjoy these homemade churros as a delightful dessert or snack! They're best enjoyed fresh and warm, straight from the frying pan.

Mexican Street Corn (Elote)

Ingredients:

- 4 ears of fresh corn, husked
- 1/4 cup mayonnaise
- 1/4 cup sour cream or Mexican crema
- 1/2 cup crumbled cotija cheese (or feta cheese can be used as a substitute)
- 1 teaspoon chili powder (adjust to taste)
- 1/2 teaspoon smoked paprika (optional)
- 1 clove garlic, minced (optional)
- 1/4 cup chopped cilantro
- Lime wedges, for serving
- Salt and pepper, to taste

Instructions:

1. **Prepare the Corn:**
    - Preheat your grill to medium-high heat, or you can use a grill pan or broiler indoors.
    - Husk the corn and remove any silk strands.
2. **Grill the Corn:**
    - Grill the corn, turning occasionally, until it is charred in spots and cooked through, about 10-12 minutes. You want some kernels to have a bit of a char for added flavor.
3. **Prepare the Creamy Mixture:**
    - In a small bowl, combine the mayonnaise, sour cream (or Mexican crema), minced garlic (if using), chili powder, smoked paprika (if using), and salt and pepper to taste. Mix well until smooth.
4. **Coat the Corn:**
    - Once the corn is grilled, brush each ear with the creamy mixture, turning to coat evenly.
5. **Add Toppings:**
    - Sprinkle each ear of corn with crumbled cotija cheese (or feta cheese), chopped cilantro, and a little more chili powder for extra spice if desired.
6. **Serve:**
    - Serve the elote immediately while still warm, with lime wedges on the side for squeezing over the corn.

Tips:

- **Variations:** Some variations include adding a squeeze of lime juice to the creamy mixture or mixing in finely chopped jalapeños for a spicy kick.

- **Cheese Substitutions:** If you can't find cotija cheese, feta cheese makes a good substitute with a similar crumbly texture and salty flavor.
- **Grilling Alternatives:** If you don't have a grill, you can also roast the corn in the oven at 400°F (200°C) for about 20-25 minutes, turning halfway through.

Mexican Street Corn (Elote) is a fantastic dish to serve as a side dish for BBQs or as a flavorful snack. Its combination of creamy, spicy, and tangy flavors makes it a favorite among both adults and kids alike. Enjoy your homemade elote!

Horchata

Ingredients:

- 1 cup long-grain white rice
- 2 cinnamon sticks
- 4 cups water
- 1/2 cup granulated sugar (adjust to taste)
- 1 teaspoon vanilla extract
- 2 cups milk (whole milk or almond milk for a dairy-free version)
- Ground cinnamon, for garnish (optional)

Instructions:

1. **Prepare the Rice and Cinnamon:**
   - Rinse the rice under cold water until the water runs clear.
   - In a blender, combine the rinsed rice, cinnamon sticks, and 2 cups of water. Blend until the rice and cinnamon sticks are broken down into a coarse mixture.
2. **Soak the Rice Mixture:**
   - Transfer the rice mixture to a large bowl and add the remaining 2 cups of water.
   - Cover the bowl and let the mixture soak at room temperature for at least 3 hours, or overnight in the refrigerator. This soaking process helps to extract maximum flavor.
3. **Blend and Strain:**
   - After soaking, blend the rice mixture again until it becomes a smooth paste.
   - Strain the blended mixture through a fine-mesh sieve or cheesecloth into a pitcher or large bowl. Use a spoon to press out as much liquid as possible.
4. **Sweeten and Flavor:**
   - Stir in the granulated sugar and vanilla extract until the sugar is completely dissolved.
   - Add the milk (or almond milk) and stir well to combine. Adjust the sweetness and thickness by adding more sugar or milk, if desired.
5. **Chill and Serve:**
   - Chill the horchata in the refrigerator for at least 1 hour before serving.
   - Stir well before serving over ice. Optionally, sprinkle ground cinnamon on top for garnish.
6. **Enjoy:**
   - Serve the horchata cold and enjoy its creamy texture and comforting cinnamon flavor.

Tips:

- **Variations:** Some recipes include almonds or other nuts for additional flavor and creaminess. You can blend soaked almonds with the rice and cinnamon or use almond milk instead of regular milk.
- **Storage:** Horchata can be stored in the refrigerator for up to 3-4 days. Stir well before serving if it separates.
- **Serve with:** Horchata pairs well with spicy foods, such as tacos or enchiladas, and is a popular drink during Mexican celebrations and gatherings.

Homemade horchata is a delightful and satisfying drink that's perfect for any occasion. Enjoy this refreshing taste of Mexican cuisine!

Arroz con Leche

Ingredients:

- 1 cup long-grain white rice
- 4 cups whole milk
- 1 cinnamon stick
- 1/2 cup granulated sugar (adjust to taste)
- 1 teaspoon vanilla extract
- Pinch of salt
- Ground cinnamon, for garnish (optional)

Instructions:

1. **Rinse and Cook the Rice:**
   - Rinse the rice under cold water until the water runs clear.
   - In a medium-sized heavy-bottomed pot, combine the rinsed rice, milk, cinnamon stick, and a pinch of salt.
2. **Simmer the Rice:**
   - Bring the mixture to a gentle boil over medium-high heat, stirring occasionally to prevent the rice from sticking to the bottom of the pot.
   - Once it boils, reduce the heat to low and let it simmer uncovered, stirring occasionally, for about 30-40 minutes or until the rice is tender and the mixture has thickened to a creamy consistency.
3. **Add Sugar and Flavorings:**
   - Stir in the granulated sugar and continue to simmer for another 5-10 minutes, stirring frequently, until the sugar is dissolved and the mixture has thickened further.
4. **Finish the Arroz con Leche:**
   - Remove the pot from the heat and stir in the vanilla extract.
   - Remove the cinnamon stick from the pot.
5. **Serve:**
   - Serve the Arroz con Leche warm or chilled. If serving chilled, let it cool to room temperature first, then refrigerate until ready to serve.
   - Optionally, sprinkle ground cinnamon on top for garnish before serving.

Tips:

- **Consistency:** The rice pudding will continue to thicken as it cools, so adjust the consistency by adding a little more milk if desired.
- **Variations:** Some recipes include condensed milk or evaporated milk for a richer flavor. You can also add raisins, nuts (such as almonds or pecans), or citrus zest for additional flavor and texture.

- **Storage:** Arroz con Leche can be stored covered in the refrigerator for up to 3-4 days. If it thickens too much upon cooling, stir in a little milk before reheating or serving.

Arroz con Leche is a comforting dessert that is perfect for both everyday enjoyment and special occasions. Its creamy texture and subtle sweetness make it a favorite in many households. Enjoy this classic dish warm or chilled, and savor its delightful flavors!

Pollo con Mole Verde

Ingredients:

- 2 lbs chicken pieces (bone-in, skin-on thighs and/or drumsticks)
- Salt and pepper, to taste
- 2 tablespoons vegetable oil
- 1 onion, chopped
- 3 garlic cloves, minced
- 1 lb fresh tomatillos, husked and rinsed
- 2-3 jalapeño or serrano peppers (adjust to taste)
- 1 cup chicken broth
- 1 cup fresh cilantro leaves
- 1/2 cup fresh parsley leaves
- 1/4 cup pumpkin seeds (pepitas), toasted
- 1/4 cup sesame seeds, toasted
- 1/2 teaspoon ground cumin
- 1/2 teaspoon ground coriander
- 1/4 teaspoon ground cloves
- 1/4 teaspoon ground cinnamon
- 1/4 teaspoon ground black pepper
- 1/2 cup sour cream or Mexican crema (optional, for finishing)
- Lime wedges, for serving
- Warm corn tortillas or rice, for serving

Instructions:

1. **Prepare the Chicken:**
    - Season the chicken pieces with salt and pepper on both sides.
2. **Brown the Chicken:**
    - In a large skillet or Dutch oven, heat the vegetable oil over medium-high heat.
    - Brown the chicken pieces on all sides until golden brown, about 5-7 minutes per side. Work in batches if necessary to avoid overcrowding the pan. Remove the chicken and set aside.
3. **Make the Mole Verde Sauce:**
    - In the same skillet or Dutch oven, add the chopped onion and cook until softened, about 3-4 minutes.
    - Add the minced garlic, tomatillos, and jalapeño or serrano peppers. Cook, stirring occasionally, until the tomatillos start to soften and release their juices, about 5 minutes.
4. **Blend the Sauce:**
    - Transfer the cooked onion, garlic, tomatillos, and peppers to a blender or food processor. Add the chicken broth, cilantro, parsley, toasted pumpkin seeds,

toasted sesame seeds, ground cumin, ground coriander, ground cloves, ground cinnamon, and ground black pepper.
    - Blend until smooth, adding more chicken broth if needed to achieve a sauce-like consistency.
5. **Simmer the Chicken in the Mole Verde:**
    - Return the browned chicken pieces to the skillet or Dutch oven.
    - Pour the blended mole verde sauce over the chicken, stirring gently to coat.
    - Bring the mixture to a simmer over medium heat. Reduce the heat to low, cover, and let it simmer gently for about 30-40 minutes, or until the chicken is cooked through and tender.
6. **Finish and Serve:**
    - Stir in the sour cream or Mexican crema, if using, to add richness and creaminess to the sauce.
    - Taste and adjust seasoning with salt and pepper if needed.
    - Serve the Pollo con Mole Verde hot, garnished with lime wedges. Accompany with warm corn tortillas or rice on the side.

Tips:

- **Toasting Seeds:** Toasting the pumpkin seeds and sesame seeds enhances their flavor. Toast them in a dry skillet over medium heat, stirring frequently until they are lightly browned and fragrant.
- **Spice Level:** Adjust the number of jalapeños or serrano peppers to your preferred level of spiciness.
- **Make-Ahead:** The mole verde sauce can be made ahead of time and stored in the refrigerator for up to 3 days or frozen for longer storage. Reheat gently on the stove before adding the chicken.
- **Variations:** Some recipes include adding greens like spinach or lettuce to the sauce for additional color and nutrition.

Pollo con Mole Verde is a wonderful dish that combines the richness of the mole verde sauce with tender chicken, creating a flavorful and satisfying meal. Enjoy this authentic Mexican dish with friends and family!

Chile Verde

Ingredients:

- 2 lbs pork shoulder or pork butt, trimmed of excess fat and cut into 1-inch cubes
- Salt and pepper, to taste
- 2 tablespoons vegetable oil
- 1 onion, chopped
- 4 cloves garlic, minced
- 2 lbs tomatillos, husked and chopped
- 2-3 jalapeño peppers, seeded and chopped (adjust to taste)
- 2 Anaheim or poblano peppers, seeded and chopped
- 1 bunch cilantro, stems removed and chopped
- 1 teaspoon ground cumin
- 1 teaspoon dried oregano
- 1/2 teaspoon ground coriander
- 2 cups chicken broth or water
- Juice of 1 lime
- Salt and pepper, to taste
- Warm tortillas, rice, and/or beans, for serving

Instructions:

1. **Prepare the Pork:**
   - Season the pork cubes with salt and pepper on all sides.
2. **Brown the Pork:**
   - In a large Dutch oven or heavy-bottomed pot, heat the vegetable oil over medium-high heat.
   - Working in batches, brown the pork cubes on all sides until golden brown. Remove the pork and set aside.
3. **Cook the Aromatics:**
   - In the same pot, add the chopped onion and cook until softened, about 3-4 minutes.
   - Add the minced garlic and cook for another 1-2 minutes until fragrant.
4. **Make the Chile Verde Sauce:**
   - Add the chopped tomatillos, jalapeño peppers, Anaheim or poblano peppers, and chopped cilantro to the pot. Cook, stirring occasionally, until the tomatillos start to break down and release their juices, about 5-7 minutes.
5. **Simmer the Chile Verde:**
   - Return the browned pork cubes to the pot along with any juices that have accumulated.
   - Stir in the ground cumin, dried oregano, and ground coriander.
   - Pour in the chicken broth or water until the pork is just covered.

- Bring the mixture to a simmer over medium heat, then reduce the heat to low. Cover and let it simmer gently for 1.5 to 2 hours, stirring occasionally, or until the pork is tender and the sauce has thickened.
6. **Finish and Serve:**
    - Stir in the lime juice and season with salt and pepper to taste.
    - Serve the Chile Verde hot, accompanied by warm tortillas, rice, and/or beans.

Tips:

- **Tomatillos:** If fresh tomatillos are not available, you can use canned tomatillos. Drain them before adding to the pot.
- **Heat Level:** Adjust the number of jalapeño peppers to your preferred level of spiciness. You can also leave some seeds in for more heat.
- **Make-Ahead:** Chile Verde tastes even better the next day, so it can be made ahead of time and reheated gently on the stove before serving.
- **Variations:** Some recipes include adding diced potatoes or green bell peppers for added texture and flavor.

Chile Verde is a hearty and satisfying dish that showcases the bright flavors of green chilies and tomatillos. It's a favorite in Mexican cuisine and sure to be enjoyed by your family and friends!

Camarones a la Diabla

Ingredients:

- 1 lb large shrimp, peeled and deveined
- Salt and pepper, to taste
- 2 tablespoons vegetable oil
- 1 onion, finely chopped
- 4 cloves garlic, minced
- 4-6 dried guajillo chilies, stemmed and seeded
- 2-3 dried arbol chilies (adjust to taste)
- 1 can (14 oz) diced tomatoes
- 1/2 cup chicken broth or water
- 1 teaspoon dried oregano
- 1/2 teaspoon ground cumin
- 1/2 teaspoon smoked paprika (optional)
- Juice of 1 lime
- Chopped cilantro, for garnish
- Lime wedges, for serving
- Warm tortillas or rice, for serving

Instructions:

1. **Prepare the Shrimp:**
   - Season the shrimp with salt and pepper.
2. **Make the Sauce:**
   - Heat 1 tablespoon of vegetable oil in a large skillet over medium-high heat.
   - Add the chopped onion and cook until softened, about 3-4 minutes.
   - Add the minced garlic and cook for another 1-2 minutes until fragrant.
3. **Prepare the Chili Sauce:**
   - In a separate skillet, heat the remaining tablespoon of vegetable oil over medium heat.
   - Add the dried guajillo chilies and arbol chilies. Toast them lightly for about 1 minute until fragrant, being careful not to burn them.
   - Transfer the toasted chilies to a blender or food processor. Add the diced tomatoes (with their juices) and chicken broth or water. Blend until smooth.
4. **Cook the Sauce:**
   - Pour the blended chili mixture into the skillet with the onions and garlic.
   - Stir in the dried oregano, ground cumin, and smoked paprika (if using).
   - Bring the sauce to a simmer and cook for about 10-15 minutes, stirring occasionally, until it thickens slightly and the flavors meld together.
5. **Add the Shrimp:**
   - Add the seasoned shrimp to the skillet with the sauce.

- Cook the shrimp for 5-7 minutes, stirring occasionally, until they are pink and opaque.
6. **Finish and Serve:**
    - Stir in the lime juice and adjust seasoning with salt and pepper if needed.
    - Garnish with chopped cilantro.
    - Serve the Camarones a la Diabla hot, accompanied by warm tortillas or rice. Serve with lime wedges on the side for squeezing over the shrimp.

Tips:

- **Adjusting Heat:** The heat level of Camarones a la Diabla can be adjusted by varying the amount of arbol chilies used. Remove the seeds for a milder dish or increase for more heat.
- **Variations:** Some recipes include adding diced potatoes, bell peppers, or carrots to the sauce along with the shrimp for added texture and flavor.
- **Side Dishes:** This dish pairs well with rice, tortillas, or crusty bread to soak up the delicious sauce. A side of refried beans and a simple salad can complement the meal nicely.

Camarones a la Diabla is a fantastic dish for those who enjoy spicy flavors. The rich chili sauce combined with tender shrimp makes for a satisfying and flavorful meal. Enjoy this traditional Mexican dish with your family and friends!

Barbacoa

Ingredients:

- 3 lbs beef chuck roast or beef cheeks, trimmed of excess fat
- Salt and pepper, to taste
- 4 cloves garlic, minced
- 1 tablespoon ground cumin
- 1 tablespoon dried oregano
- 1 teaspoon smoked paprika (optional)
- 1 teaspoon ground cloves
- 1/2 teaspoon ground cinnamon
- 1/4 teaspoon ground cayenne pepper (adjust to taste)
- 1/2 cup beef broth or water
- 1/4 cup apple cider vinegar or white vinegar
- Juice of 2 limes
- Corn or flour tortillas, for serving
- Chopped cilantro, diced onions, lime wedges, and salsa, for serving

Instructions:

1. **Prepare the Beef:**
    - Season the beef chuck roast or beef cheeks generously with salt and pepper.
2. **Make the Barbacoa Marinade:**
    - In a small bowl, combine the minced garlic, ground cumin, dried oregano, smoked paprika (if using), ground cloves, ground cinnamon, and ground cayenne pepper.
    - Rub the marinade mixture evenly all over the seasoned beef. Let it marinate for at least 30 minutes at room temperature, or cover and refrigerate overnight for deeper flavor.
3. **Cook the Barbacoa:**
    - Preheat your oven to 325°F (165°C).
    - Place the marinated beef in a Dutch oven or heavy-bottomed pot with a lid.
    - Pour in the beef broth (or water), apple cider vinegar (or white vinegar), and lime juice around the beef.
4. **Slow Cook the Barbacoa:**
    - Cover the Dutch oven with the lid and transfer it to the preheated oven.
    - Bake for 3-4 hours, or until the beef is tender and easily pulls apart with a fork. Check halfway through and add more liquid if needed to prevent drying out.
5. **Shred the Barbacoa:**
    - Once the beef is tender, remove it from the oven and transfer it to a cutting board.
    - Use two forks to shred the beef into smaller pieces. It should be very tender and easily shredable.

6. **Serve the Barbacoa:**
   - Serve the shredded barbacoa beef warm, wrapped in warm corn or flour tortillas.
   - Garnish with chopped cilantro, diced onions, and serve with lime wedges and salsa on the side.

Tips:

- **Variations:** Some recipes include adding chopped onions, bay leaves, or chipotle peppers in adobo sauce for additional flavor. Feel free to adjust the seasonings and spices to your preference.
- **Storage:** Leftover barbacoa can be stored in an airtight container in the refrigerator for up to 3-4 days. It also freezes well for longer storage.
- **Serving Suggestions:** Barbacoa is traditionally served with warm tortillas and accompanied by chopped onions, cilantro, lime wedges, and salsa. It also pairs well with rice, beans, or grilled vegetables.

Barbacoa is a delicious and versatile dish that's perfect for gatherings or as a flavorful meal any day of the week. Enjoy the rich, tender beef with its aromatic spices and traditional accompaniments!

Papas con Chorizo

Ingredients:

- 4 medium potatoes, peeled and diced into small cubes
- 1 tablespoon vegetable oil
- 1/2 lb fresh Mexican chorizo sausage, casing removed
- 1/2 onion, finely chopped
- 2 cloves garlic, minced
- 1 jalapeño or serrano pepper, seeded and finely chopped (optional, for heat)
- 1 tomato, diced
- 1/2 teaspoon ground cumin
- Salt and pepper, to taste
- 1/4 cup chopped cilantro, for garnish (optional)
- Warm corn or flour tortillas, for serving

Instructions:

1. **Prepare the Potatoes:**
   - Peel the potatoes and dice them into small cubes.
2. **Cook the Potatoes:**
   - Heat the vegetable oil in a large skillet over medium heat.
   - Add the diced potatoes to the skillet and season with salt and pepper.
   - Cook the potatoes, stirring occasionally, until they are golden brown and tender, about 10-12 minutes. Remove the potatoes from the skillet and set aside.
3. **Cook the Chorizo:**
   - In the same skillet, add the Mexican chorizo sausage (casing removed) and break it up with a spatula.
   - Cook the chorizo over medium heat, stirring occasionally, until it is fully cooked and browned, about 5-7 minutes.
4. **Combine Ingredients:**
   - Add the chopped onion, minced garlic, and chopped jalapeño or serrano pepper (if using) to the skillet with the cooked chorizo. Cook, stirring occasionally, until the onions are translucent, about 3-4 minutes.
5. **Add Tomatoes and Seasonings:**
   - Stir in the diced tomato and ground cumin. Cook for another 2-3 minutes until the tomato starts to soften.
6. **Finish Papas con Chorizo:**
   - Return the cooked potatoes to the skillet with the chorizo mixture. Stir well to combine all ingredients.
   - Cook for an additional 2-3 minutes, stirring occasionally, to allow the flavors to meld together.
   - Taste and adjust seasoning with salt and pepper if needed.
7. **Serve:**

- Serve Papas con Chorizo hot, garnished with chopped cilantro if desired.
- Serve with warm corn or flour tortillas on the side for scooping up the delicious mixture.

Tips:

- **Variations:** You can add diced bell peppers or chopped spinach to the dish for added flavor and nutrition.
- **Spice Level:** Adjust the amount of jalapeño or serrano pepper to your preferred level of spiciness.
- **Make-Ahead:** Papas con Chorizo can be made ahead of time and reheated gently on the stove or in the microwave before serving.

Papas con Chorizo is a comforting and satisfying dish that's perfect for any meal of the day. Enjoy its bold flavors and versatility!

Sopes

Ingredients:

- 2 cups masa harina (corn flour)
- 1 1/4 cups warm water
- 1/2 teaspoon salt
- Vegetable oil, for frying
- Toppings of your choice, such as:
    - Refried beans
    - Shredded chicken or beef
    - Chopped lettuce or cabbage
    - Diced tomatoes
    - Crumbled cheese (queso fresco or cotija)
    - Salsa (red or green)
    - Sour cream or Mexican crema
    - Sliced avocado
    - Chopped cilantro

Instructions:

1. **Prepare the Masa Dough:**
    - In a large mixing bowl, combine the masa harina and salt.
    - Gradually add the warm water while mixing with your hands until the dough comes together and is smooth and pliable. It should feel like Play-Doh consistency. If it's too dry, add a bit more water; if too wet, add a little more masa harina.
2. **Form the Sopes:**
    - Pinch off a golf ball-sized piece of dough and roll it into a ball. Flatten it slightly between your palms to form a thick disk, about 1/4 to 1/2 inch thick.
    - Use your thumbs to press an indentation in the center of the disk, creating a rim or border around the edge. This helps to contain the toppings.
3. **Fry the Sopes:**
    - Heat about 1/2 inch of vegetable oil in a large skillet or frying pan over medium-high heat until hot but not smoking.
    - Carefully place the formed sopes into the hot oil, working in batches if necessary to avoid overcrowding.
    - Fry each side for about 2-3 minutes, or until golden brown and crispy. Use tongs to flip them halfway through frying.
    - Remove the sopes from the oil and place them on paper towels to drain excess oil.
4. **Assemble the Sopes:**
    - Once all sopes are fried and drained, top each one with your desired toppings.

- Start with a layer of refried beans, followed by shredded meat (if using), lettuce or cabbage, diced tomatoes, crumbled cheese, salsa, sour cream or Mexican crema, sliced avocado, and chopped cilantro.
5. **Serve:**
   - Arrange the prepared sopes on a serving platter and serve immediately while still warm.

Tips:

- **Variations:** Sopes can be customized with a wide range of toppings to suit your preferences. Experiment with different combinations of meats, vegetables, cheeses, and salsas.
- **Preparation:** You can prepare the masa dough and shape the sopes ahead of time. Fry them just before serving to ensure they stay crispy.
- **Storage:** If you have leftover sopes, store the unfried dough in an airtight container in the refrigerator for up to 2 days. Fry them fresh as needed.

Sopes are a delightful and versatile dish that can be enjoyed as appetizers, snacks, or even a light meal. Their crispy exterior and soft interior, paired with flavorful toppings, make them a favorite in Mexican cuisine. Enjoy making and savoring these homemade sopes with your favorite toppings!

Aguachile

Ingredients:

- 1 lb fresh raw shrimp, peeled and deveined
- 1 cup fresh lime juice (about 8-10 limes)
- 1/2 cup cold water
- 2-3 serrano chilies (or more, depending on desired spiciness), thinly sliced
- 1/2 red onion, thinly sliced
- 1 cucumber, peeled and thinly sliced
- 1/4 cup chopped cilantro
- Salt, to taste
- Tortilla chips or tostadas, for serving (optional)

Instructions:

1. **Prepare the Shrimp:**
   - Rinse the shrimp under cold water and pat dry with paper towels. Cut each shrimp in half lengthwise (optional).
2. **Make the Aguachile Sauce:**
   - In a large bowl, combine the lime juice, cold water, and sliced serrano chilies. Stir to mix well.
   - Taste the mixture and adjust the amount of serrano chilies based on your desired level of spiciness.
3. **Marinate the Shrimp:**
   - Add the raw shrimp to the bowl with the lime juice mixture. Make sure the shrimp are fully submerged in the liquid.
   - Cover the bowl with plastic wrap and refrigerate for about 15-20 minutes. The acid in the lime juice will "cook" the shrimp, turning them opaque and firm.
4. **Assemble Aguachile:**
   - After marinating, remove the shrimp from the lime juice mixture and transfer them to a serving bowl or platter.
   - Strain the lime juice mixture to remove the sliced serrano chilies (you can leave some in if you prefer extra heat).
   - Pour the strained lime juice mixture over the shrimp.
5. **Add Toppings:**
   - Scatter the thinly sliced red onion and cucumber over the shrimp.
   - Sprinkle chopped cilantro on top.
   - Season lightly with salt, if needed (depending on how salty your lime juice mixture is).
6. **Serve:**
   - Serve Aguachile immediately as a refreshing appetizer or main dish.
   - Optionally, serve with tortilla chips or tostadas on the side to scoop up the shrimp and sauce.

Tips:

- **Freshness:** Aguachile is best enjoyed immediately after assembling to maintain the freshness and texture of the shrimp.
- **Variations:** Some recipes include adding diced avocado or mango for added creaminess or sweetness.
- **Storage:** Aguachile is meant to be served fresh due to the raw nature of the shrimp. Consume leftovers promptly and store in the refrigerator for no more than a day.

Aguachile is a vibrant and zesty dish that showcases the fresh flavors of seafood and citrus. It's perfect for warm weather or as a starter to a Mexican-inspired meal. Enjoy the bold and refreshing taste of homemade Aguachile!

Caldo de Res

Ingredients:

- 2 lbs beef shank or beef stew meat, cut into chunks
- 8 cups beef broth or water
- 2 cloves garlic, minced
- 1 onion, chopped
- 2 tomatoes, diced
- 2 carrots, peeled and sliced
- 2 potatoes, peeled and cut into chunks
- 2 ears of corn, cut into thirds (or 1 cup frozen corn)
- 2 chayotes, peeled and cut into chunks (optional)
- 1 zucchini, sliced
- 1/2 cabbage, sliced into wedges
- 1 bay leaf
- 1 teaspoon dried oregano
- Salt and pepper, to taste
- Fresh cilantro, chopped, for garnish
- Lime wedges, for serving
- Warm corn tortillas, for serving

Instructions:

1. **Prepare the Beef:**
   - In a large pot or Dutch oven, combine the beef shank or beef stew meat with the beef broth or water.
   - Bring to a boil over medium-high heat, then reduce the heat to low. Skim off any foam that rises to the surface.
2. **Simmer the Beef:**
   - Add the minced garlic, chopped onion, and diced tomatoes to the pot.
   - Cover and simmer gently for about 1.5 to 2 hours, or until the beef is tender. Stir occasionally and check for tenderness.
3. **Add Vegetables:**
   - Once the beef is tender, add the sliced carrots, potatoes, corn, and chayotes (if using) to the pot.
   - Simmer for another 15-20 minutes, or until the vegetables are tender.
4. **Add Zucchini and Cabbage:**
   - Add the sliced zucchini and cabbage wedges to the pot.
   - Continue to simmer for another 10 minutes, or until the zucchini is tender and the cabbage is softened.
5. **Season and Serve:**
   - Stir in the bay leaf and dried oregano. Season with salt and pepper to taste.
   - Remove the bay leaf before serving.

6. **Serve:**
    - Ladle the Caldo de Res into bowls. Garnish with chopped fresh cilantro.
    - Serve with lime wedges on the side for squeezing over the soup.
    - Serve warm with warm corn tortillas on the side.

Tips:

- **Variations:** Some recipes include adding green beans, celery, or other favorite vegetables. Adjust the vegetables based on personal preference.
- **Storage:** Caldo de Res can be stored in an airtight container in the refrigerator for up to 3-4 days. Reheat gently on the stove before serving.
- **Serving Suggestions:** This soup is hearty enough to be a meal on its own, but it's also common to serve it with rice or warm tortillas on the side.

Caldo de Res is a comforting and nourishing soup that's perfect for chilly days or whenever you crave a hearty meal. Enjoy the rich flavors and textures of this traditional Mexican beef soup!

Molletes

Ingredients:

- 4 bolillo rolls (or substitute with French bread or baguette)
- 1 can (16 oz) refried beans
- 1 cup shredded cheese (traditionally Oaxaca cheese, Monterey Jack, or mozzarella)
- Salsa, for serving (optional)
- Sliced avocado, for serving (optional)
- Chopped cilantro, for garnish (optional)

Instructions:

1. **Prepare the Bolillo Rolls:**
   - Preheat your oven to 350°F (175°C).
   - Slice the bolillo rolls in half horizontally to create top and bottom halves.
2. **Toast the Bolillo Halves:**
   - Place the bolillo halves cut-side up on a baking sheet.
   - Toast them in the preheated oven for about 5-7 minutes, or until they are lightly toasted. This step helps to crisp up the bread slightly.
3. **Prepare the Refried Beans:**
   - While the bolillo halves are toasting, heat the refried beans in a small saucepan over medium heat until warmed through. You can add a splash of water or broth if needed to loosen the beans.
4. **Assemble the Molletes:**
   - Once the bolillo halves are toasted, spread a generous layer of warm refried beans on each half.
   - Sprinkle shredded cheese evenly over the beans.
5. **Broil the Molletes:**
   - Set your oven to broil (high).
   - Place the assembled molletes back into the oven and broil for 2-3 minutes, or until the cheese is melted and bubbly. Keep a close eye on them to prevent burning.
6. **Serve:**
   - Remove the molletes from the oven and transfer them to a serving platter.
   - Serve immediately, garnished with salsa, sliced avocado, and chopped cilantro if desired.

Tips:

- **Variations:** You can customize molletes by adding toppings like cooked chorizo, ham slices, or pickled jalapeños before melting the cheese.
- **Bread Substitutions:** If bolillo rolls are not available, you can use French bread or baguette as a substitute.

- **Make-Ahead:** You can prepare the bolillo halves and warm the refried beans ahead of time. Assemble and broil the molletes just before serving for best results.

Molletes are simple yet flavorful, making them a versatile dish that can be enjoyed for breakfast, brunch, lunch, or even as a snack. They're a delightful example of Mexican comfort food that's easy to prepare at home. Enjoy your homemade molletes with your favorite toppings and savor the cheesy, bean-filled goodness!

Empanadas

Dough Ingredients:

- 3 cups all-purpose flour
- 1/2 teaspoon salt
- 1/2 cup (1 stick) unsalted butter, chilled and cut into cubes
- 1 large egg
- 1/2 cup cold water

Filling Ingredients (Beef Empanadas):

- 1 lb ground beef
- 1 small onion, finely chopped
- 2 cloves garlic, minced
- 1 teaspoon ground cumin
- 1 teaspoon paprika
- 1/2 teaspoon dried oregano
- Salt and pepper, to taste
- 1/2 cup green olives, pitted and chopped (optional)
- 2 hard-boiled eggs, chopped (optional)
- 1/2 cup raisins (optional)
- Vegetable oil, for frying (if frying)

Instructions:

1. Prepare the Dough:

1. In a large mixing bowl, whisk together the flour and salt.
2. Add the chilled cubed butter to the flour mixture. Using a pastry cutter or your fingers, work the butter into the flour until the mixture resembles coarse crumbs.
3. In a small bowl, beat the egg with cold water. Gradually add the egg mixture to the flour mixture, stirring with a fork until the dough comes together. You may not need to use all of the egg mixture.
4. Turn the dough out onto a lightly floured surface and knead gently until smooth. Shape the dough into a ball, wrap it in plastic wrap, and refrigerate for at least 30 minutes (or up to 24 hours) to allow it to rest.

2. Prepare the Filling:

1. In a skillet, cook the ground beef over medium-high heat until browned and cooked through, breaking it up with a spoon as it cooks.
2. Add the chopped onion and garlic to the skillet with the ground beef. Cook for 2-3 minutes until the onion is translucent.

3. Stir in the ground cumin, paprika, dried oregano, salt, and pepper. Cook for another minute until the spices are fragrant.
4. Remove the skillet from heat and stir in the chopped green olives, hard-boiled eggs (if using), and raisins (if using). Let the filling mixture cool completely before assembling the empanadas.

3. Assemble the Empanadas:

1. Preheat your oven to 375°F (190°C) if baking the empanadas. Line a baking sheet with parchment paper.
2. Divide the chilled dough into about 12 equal portions. Roll each portion into a ball and then flatten it into a disk about 5-6 inches in diameter.
3. Place a spoonful of the cooled filling in the center of each dough disk. Be careful not to overfill.
4. Fold the dough over the filling to create a half-moon shape. Use a fork to press and seal the edges firmly. You can also crimp the edges decoratively with your fingers.
5. If baking, place the assembled empanadas on the prepared baking sheet. Brush the tops with beaten egg for a shiny finish.
6. If frying, heat vegetable oil in a deep skillet or pot until it reaches 350°F (175°C). Fry the empanadas in batches until golden brown on both sides, about 3-4 minutes per side. Transfer to a paper towel-lined plate to drain excess oil.

4. Bake or Fry the Empanadas:

- **Baking:** Bake the empanadas in the preheated oven for 20-25 minutes, or until golden brown and crispy.
- **Frying:** Fry the empanadas in batches until golden brown and crispy on both sides. Drain on paper towels.

5. Serve:

- Serve the empanadas warm as a delicious appetizer, snack, or meal. They can be served with salsa, chimichurri sauce, or a simple salad on the side.

Tips:

- **Variations:** Empanadas can be filled with a variety of ingredients such as chicken, cheese, spinach, or even sweet fillings like fruit or dulce de leche.
- **Storage:** Store leftover empanadas in an airtight container in the refrigerator for up to 3 days. Reheat in the oven or microwave before serving.
- **Make-Ahead:** You can prepare the dough and filling ahead of time and assemble the empanadas just before baking or frying.

Enjoy these homemade empanadas filled with flavorful beef and spices, wrapped in a crispy golden pastry shell. They are perfect for sharing with family and friends, and sure to be a hit at any gathering!

Camotes Enmielados

Ingredients:

- 4 medium sweet potatoes
- 1 cone of piloncillo (about 8 oz), or substitute with 1 cup of packed brown sugar
- 1 cinnamon stick
- 1 orange or lime, zest only (optional)
- Water, enough to cover the sweet potatoes

Instructions:

1. **Prepare the Sweet Potatoes:**
   - Peel the sweet potatoes and cut them into thick rounds or chunks, about 1 to 1.5 inches thick.
2. **Make the Syrup:**
   - In a large pot, combine the piloncillo cone (or brown sugar), cinnamon stick, and citrus zest (if using).
   - Add enough water to cover the sweet potatoes by about 1 inch.
3. **Cook the Sweet Potatoes:**
   - Bring the syrup mixture to a boil over medium-high heat, stirring occasionally to dissolve the piloncillo (or brown sugar).
4. **Add the Sweet Potatoes:**
   - Carefully add the sweet potato chunks to the pot with the boiling syrup.
5. **Simmer:**
   - Reduce the heat to medium-low and simmer gently, uncovered, for about 30-40 minutes, or until the sweet potatoes are tender and the syrup has thickened and become slightly caramelized.
   - Stir occasionally to coat the sweet potatoes evenly with the syrup.
6. **Serve:**
   - Once the sweet potatoes are tender and the syrup has thickened, remove the pot from heat.
   - Let the camotes enmielados cool slightly before serving.
7. **Optional Garnish:**
   - Serve the camotes enmielados warm or at room temperature.
   - Optionally, garnish with additional cinnamon sticks or citrus zest for decoration.

Tips:

- **Variations:** Some recipes include adding a pinch of ground cloves or nutmeg for extra flavor. You can also add a splash of vanilla extract or a small piece of Mexican cinnamon (canela) for a different twist.
- **Storage:** Camotes enmielados can be stored in the refrigerator in an airtight container for up to 3-4 days. Reheat gently on the stove or in the microwave before serving.

- **Serving Suggestions:** Enjoy camotes enmielados as a dessert or sweet snack. They are often served on their own, but you can also pair them with vanilla ice cream or whipped cream for a decadent treat.

Camotes enmielados are a wonderful way to enjoy sweet potatoes with a touch of Mexican flair. The combination of sweet, caramelized syrup with tender sweet potatoes creates a delightful and comforting dessert that's perfect for cooler weather or any time you crave something sweet and satisfying.

Pescado a la Veracruzana

Ingredients:

- 4 fillets of firm white fish (such as red snapper, grouper, or tilapia), about 6-8 oz each
- Salt and pepper, to taste
- All-purpose flour, for dredging
- 3 tablespoons olive oil
- 1 onion, thinly sliced
- 2 cloves garlic, minced
- 1 bell pepper (red or green), thinly sliced
- 2 tomatoes, diced (or 1 can diced tomatoes, drained)
- 1/4 cup green olives, sliced
- 2 tablespoons capers, drained
- 1/2 teaspoon dried oregano
- 1/2 teaspoon dried thyme
- 1/2 cup fish or vegetable broth
- 1/4 cup white wine (optional)
- Fresh cilantro or parsley, chopped, for garnish
- Lime wedges, for serving
- Cooked rice or warm tortillas, for serving

Instructions:

1. **Prepare the Fish:**
   - Pat the fish fillets dry with paper towels. Season both sides with salt and pepper.
   - Lightly dredge the fish fillets in flour, shaking off any excess.
2. **Sear the Fish:**
   - Heat 2 tablespoons of olive oil in a large skillet over medium-high heat.
   - Add the fish fillets and cook for about 2-3 minutes per side, or until golden brown and cooked through. Remove the fish from the skillet and set aside.
3. **Make the Veracruzana Sauce:**
   - In the same skillet, heat the remaining 1 tablespoon of olive oil over medium heat.
   - Add the sliced onion and bell pepper. Cook, stirring occasionally, until softened, about 5-7 minutes.
4. **Add Aromatics and Tomatoes:**
   - Stir in the minced garlic and cook for another 1-2 minutes until fragrant.
   - Add the diced tomatoes (or canned tomatoes) to the skillet, along with the green olives, capers, dried oregano, and dried thyme. Cook for 5 minutes, stirring occasionally.
5. **Simmer the Sauce:**

- Pour in the fish or vegetable broth and white wine (if using). Bring the mixture to a simmer and cook for another 5-7 minutes, or until the sauce has slightly thickened.

6. **Combine and Finish:**
   - Return the cooked fish fillets to the skillet, nestling them into the sauce. Spoon some of the sauce over the top of the fish.
   - Cover the skillet and simmer gently for 5 minutes to allow the flavors to meld together and to ensure the fish is heated through.

7. **Serve:**
   - Transfer the Pescado a la Veracruzana to a serving platter or individual plates.
   - Garnish with chopped fresh cilantro or parsley.
   - Serve with lime wedges on the side for squeezing over the fish.
   - Enjoy Pescado a la Veracruzana with cooked rice or warm tortillas.

Tips:

- **Variations:** You can adjust the spiciness of the dish by adding more or fewer chili peppers. Some recipes also include a splash of vinegar or Worcestershire sauce for added depth of flavor.
- **Substitutions:** If you prefer, you can use canned green chilies instead of fresh bell peppers.
- **Serving Suggestions:** Pescado a la Veracruzana is traditionally served with rice to soak up the delicious sauce. It also pairs well with warm tortillas for a more casual meal.

Pescado a la Veracruzana is a vibrant and aromatic dish that showcases the flavors of Mexico's coastal cuisine. It's perfect for seafood lovers and those looking to explore traditional Mexican flavors at home. Enjoy this flavorful dish with family and friends!

Cochinita Pibil Tacos

Ingredients:

For the Cochinita Pibil:

- 2 lbs pork shoulder or pork butt, cut into chunks
- 1/2 cup achiote paste
- 1/2 cup orange juice (preferably freshly squeezed)
- 1/4 cup lime juice (preferably freshly squeezed)
- 3 cloves garlic, minced
- 1 teaspoon ground cumin
- 1 teaspoon dried oregano
- 1/2 teaspoon ground cloves
- Salt, to taste
- Banana leaves or aluminum foil (for wrapping, optional)

For Serving:

- Corn tortillas, warmed
- Pickled red onions (optional, for garnish)
- Fresh cilantro, chopped (for garnish)
- Salsa or hot sauce (optional, for serving)

Instructions:

1. **Marinate the Pork:**
   - In a large bowl, combine the achiote paste, orange juice, lime juice, minced garlic, ground cumin, dried oregano, ground cloves, and salt. Mix well to form a marinade.
   - Add the pork chunks to the marinade, making sure each piece is well coated. Cover and refrigerate for at least 4 hours, preferably overnight, to allow the flavors to meld.
2. **Cook the Cochinita Pibil:**
   - Preheat your oven to 325°F (160°C).
   - If using banana leaves (traditional), briefly pass them over an open flame to soften and make them pliable. Alternatively, you can use aluminum foil.
   - Place the marinated pork and marinade in a baking dish lined with banana leaves or aluminum foil. Wrap the pork tightly in the leaves or foil, ensuring it's well-sealed.
   - Bake in the preheated oven for 3-4 hours, or until the pork is very tender and easily pulls apart with a fork. If using a slow cooker, cook on low for 6-8 hours.
3. **Shred the Pork:**
   - Once the pork is cooked, remove it from the oven or slow cooker. Carefully unwrap the banana leaves or foil.

- Use two forks to shred the pork into smaller pieces. Mix the shredded pork with the cooking juices to keep it moist and flavorful.

4. **Assemble the Tacos:**
   - Warm the corn tortillas in a dry skillet or on a griddle until they are pliable and slightly charred.
   - Spoon some of the cochinita pibil onto each tortilla. Top with pickled red onions (if using) and chopped fresh cilantro.
   - Serve immediately with salsa or hot sauce on the side, if desired.

Tips:

- **Achiote Paste:** Achiote paste is a key ingredient that gives cochinita pibil its distinctive red color and flavor. It can usually be found in Latin American grocery stores or online. If you can't find it, you can make a substitute with annatto powder, vinegar, and other spices.
- **Banana Leaves:** While traditional, banana leaves can be optional. They add a subtle flavor and help keep the pork moist during cooking. If unavailable, aluminum foil works well for baking.
- **Make-Ahead:** Cochinita pibil can be made ahead of time and reheated before serving. It often tastes even better the next day as the flavors continue to develop.

Cochinita Pibil Tacos are a festive and flavorful dish that showcases the rich culinary heritage of the Yucatán region. The tender, citrus-infused pork paired with tangy pickled onions and fresh cilantro makes for a satisfying and delicious taco experience. Enjoy these tacos for a special occasion or any time you crave authentic Mexican flavors!

Tlacoyos

Ingredients:

For the Masa (Dough):

- 2 cups masa harina (corn flour for tortillas, such as Maseca)
- 1 1/4 cups warm water
- 1/2 teaspoon salt

For the Filling:

- 1 cup refried beans (or black beans, cooked and mashed)
- 1/2 cup crumbled queso fresco or shredded cheese (optional)
- Salsa or hot sauce, for serving (optional)
- Chopped onion, cilantro, and lime wedges, for garnish (optional)

For Cooking:

- Vegetable oil or cooking spray

Instructions:

1. **Prepare the Masa Dough:**
    - In a large mixing bowl, combine the masa harina and salt.
    - Gradually add the warm water, mixing with your hands or a wooden spoon, until a smooth dough forms. The dough should be soft and slightly sticky. If it feels too dry, add a little more water; if too wet, add a bit more masa harina.
2. **Form the Tlacoyos:**
    - Divide the masa dough into 8 equal portions. Roll each portion into a ball.
    - Flatten each ball into an oval shape, about 4-5 inches long and 2-3 inches wide. Use your fingers to create a shallow well in the center of each oval, making sure not to tear through the dough.
3. **Fill and Shape the Tlacoyos:**
    - Spoon a tablespoon or two of refried beans (or other filling of your choice) into the center of each masa oval.
    - Fold the masa over the filling, pinching the edges together to seal and form an oval shape. Gently flatten the tlacoyo slightly with your hands, making sure the filling is evenly distributed and the dough is sealed.
4. **Cook the Tlacoyos:**
    - Heat a non-stick skillet or griddle over medium heat and lightly grease it with vegetable oil or cooking spray.
    - Place the filled tlacoyos on the hot skillet and cook for about 3-4 minutes on each side, or until they are golden brown and slightly crispy. You may need to adjust the heat to ensure they cook through without burning.

5. **Serve:**
    - Remove the cooked tlacoyos from the skillet and transfer them to a serving platter.
    - Serve warm, garnished with crumbled queso fresco or shredded cheese, salsa or hot sauce, chopped onion, cilantro, and lime wedges on the side.

Tips:

- **Variations:** Tlacoyos can be filled with a variety of ingredients, such as cooked shredded chicken, chorizo, or even mashed potatoes. Get creative with your fillings!
- **Make-Ahead:** You can prepare the masa dough and fill the tlacoyos ahead of time, storing them covered in the refrigerator until ready to cook. Cooked tlacoyos can also be stored in the refrigerator and reheated in a skillet or microwave.
- **Serving Suggestions:** Tlacoyos are delicious on their own as a snack or appetizer, or they can be served alongside Mexican rice and beans for a more substantial meal.

Tlacoyos are a wonderful representation of traditional Mexican cuisine, showcasing the versatility of masa dough and the deliciousness of savory fillings. Enjoy making and savoring these homemade tlacoyos with your favorite toppings!

Camarones al Mojo de Ajo

Ingredients:

- 1 lb large shrimp, peeled and deveined
- 6 cloves garlic, minced
- 1/2 cup unsalted butter
- 1/4 cup olive oil
- 1/4 cup chopped fresh parsley
- 1/2 teaspoon dried oregano
- 1/4 teaspoon red pepper flakes (optional, for a bit of heat)
- Salt and black pepper, to taste
- Lime wedges, for serving
- Warm tortillas or rice, for serving

Instructions:

1. **Prepare the Shrimp:**
   - If the shrimp are not already peeled and deveined, peel them and remove the veins. Rinse the shrimp under cold water and pat dry with paper towels.
2. **Cook the Garlic Butter Sauce:**
   - In a large skillet or pan, heat the olive oil and butter over medium heat until the butter is melted.
   - Add the minced garlic to the skillet and cook for 1-2 minutes, stirring frequently, until the garlic is fragrant and just beginning to brown. Be careful not to burn the garlic.
3. **Cook the Shrimp:**
   - Increase the heat to medium-high and add the shrimp to the skillet in a single layer. Season with salt, black pepper, dried oregano, and red pepper flakes (if using).
   - Cook the shrimp for 2-3 minutes per side, or until they are pink and opaque. Stir occasionally to ensure even cooking. Be careful not to overcook the shrimp, as they can become tough.
4. **Finish and Serve:**
   - Once the shrimp are cooked through, sprinkle chopped fresh parsley over them and toss to combine, allowing the flavors to meld together.
   - Remove the skillet from heat and serve the Camarones al Mojo de Ajo immediately.
5. **Serve:**
   - Serve the garlic butter shrimp hot, garnished with additional parsley if desired, and with lime wedges on the side for squeezing over the shrimp.
   - Camarones al Mojo de Ajo are traditionally served with warm tortillas for making tacos or with rice on the side. They make a delicious and satisfying main dish or appetizer.

Tips:

- **Variations:** You can customize this dish by adding sliced jalapeños or bell peppers to the garlic butter sauce for extra flavor and color.
- **Garlic:** Adjust the amount of garlic according to your preference. If you love garlic, feel free to add more cloves for a stronger garlic flavor.
- **Serving Suggestions:** This dish pairs well with a fresh salad, Mexican-style rice, or grilled vegetables. It's also great served over pasta for a different twist.

Camarones al Mojo de Ajo is a delightful dish that highlights the vibrant flavors of garlic and butter with tender shrimp. It's perfect for a quick weeknight meal or for entertaining guests. Enjoy the rich and savory taste of this classic Mexican seafood recipe!

Guajillo Chicken

Ingredients:

- 4 boneless, skinless chicken breasts or thighs
- 4-5 guajillo chilies, stems and seeds removed
- 2 tomatoes, chopped
- 1 onion, chopped
- 4 cloves garlic, minced
- 1 teaspoon dried oregano
- 1/2 teaspoon ground cumin
- 1/2 teaspoon ground cloves
- 1/2 teaspoon ground cinnamon
- Salt and pepper, to taste
- 2 cups chicken broth
- 2 tablespoons vegetable oil
- Fresh cilantro, chopped, for garnish (optional)
- Lime wedges, for serving

Instructions:

1. **Prepare the Guajillo Sauce:**
   - Heat a dry skillet or comal over medium heat. Toast the guajillo chilies for about 1-2 minutes per side, until they become fragrant and slightly softened. Be careful not to burn them.
   - Remove the chilies from the skillet and transfer them to a bowl. Cover them with hot water and let them soak for about 15-20 minutes, until they are softened.
2. **Blend the Sauce:**
   - In a blender or food processor, combine the soaked guajillo chilies (drained), chopped tomatoes, chopped onion, minced garlic, dried oregano, ground cumin, ground cloves, ground cinnamon, salt, and pepper.
   - Add 1 cup of chicken broth to the blender and blend until you have a smooth sauce. If needed, add more chicken broth to achieve the desired consistency. Strain the sauce through a fine mesh sieve to remove any solids, if desired.
3. **Cook the Chicken:**
   - Season the chicken breasts or thighs with salt and pepper on both sides.
   - In a large skillet or Dutch oven, heat the vegetable oil over medium-high heat. Brown the chicken on both sides until golden, about 3-4 minutes per side. Remove the chicken from the skillet and set it aside.
4. **Simmer the Guajillo Sauce:**
   - Pour the blended guajillo sauce into the skillet. Bring it to a simmer over medium heat.
   - Add the browned chicken back into the skillet, nestling it into the sauce.
   - Pour in the remaining 1 cup of chicken broth, enough to cover the chicken partially. Bring the mixture to a simmer.
5. **Finish Cooking:**

- Reduce the heat to low, cover the skillet, and let the chicken simmer gently for 20-25 minutes, or until the chicken is cooked through and tender. The internal temperature of the chicken should reach 165°F (75°C).

6. **Serve:**
    - Once the chicken is cooked, remove it from the skillet and place it on a serving platter.
    - Spoon some of the guajillo sauce over the chicken. Garnish with chopped fresh cilantro, if desired.
    - Serve Guajillo Chicken hot, with lime wedges on the side for squeezing over the chicken. It pairs well with rice, beans, or warm tortillas.

Tips:

- **Adjust Heat Level:** Guajillo chilies are mild in heat. For a spicier dish, you can add a couple of arbol chilies or adjust the amount of guajillo chilies to your preference.
- **Make-Ahead:** You can prepare the guajillo sauce ahead of time and store it in the refrigerator for up to 3 days. Cook the chicken and finish the dish when ready to serve.
- **Variations:** Feel free to add sliced bell peppers, potatoes, or carrots to the dish along with the chicken for a heartier meal.

Guajillo Chicken is a comforting and flavorful dish that showcases the rich flavors of Mexican cuisine. Enjoy the tender chicken infused with the smoky and tangy guajillo sauce for a satisfying meal that's sure to impress!

Pan de Elote

Ingredients:

- 4 ears of corn, kernels removed (about 2 cups of corn kernels)
- 1/2 cup unsalted butter, melted
- 1/2 cup granulated sugar
- 3 large eggs
- 1 teaspoon vanilla extract
- 1/2 cup all-purpose flour
- 1/2 cup cornmeal
- 1 teaspoon baking powder
- 1/4 teaspoon salt
- 1/2 cup milk
- Powdered sugar, for dusting (optional)

Instructions:

1. **Prepare the Corn:**
   - Preheat your oven to 350°F (175°C). Grease and flour a 9-inch round cake pan or an 8x8-inch baking dish.
   - If using fresh corn, cut the kernels off the cobs until you have about 2 cups. You can also use canned or frozen corn kernels (thawed and drained).
2. **Blend the Ingredients:**
   - In a blender or food processor, combine the corn kernels, melted butter, and granulated sugar. Blend until smooth.
   - Add the eggs and vanilla extract to the blender. Blend again until well combined.
3. **Mix the Dry Ingredients:**
   - In a separate bowl, whisk together the flour, cornmeal, baking powder, and salt.
4. **Combine Wet and Dry Ingredients:**
   - Pour the blended corn mixture into the bowl with the dry ingredients. Stir gently until just combined.
   - Gradually add the milk, stirring until the batter is smooth and well mixed.
5. **Bake the Pan de Elote:**
   - Pour the batter into the prepared cake pan or baking dish, spreading it evenly.
   - Bake in the preheated oven for 40-45 minutes, or until the top is golden brown and a toothpick inserted into the center comes out clean.
6. **Cool and Serve:**
   - Remove the Pan de Elote from the oven and let it cool in the pan for about 10 minutes.
   - Once cooled slightly, transfer the Pan de Elote to a wire rack to cool completely.
7. **Serve:**
   - Dust the Pan de Elote with powdered sugar, if desired, before serving.
   - Slice and serve the Pan de Elote warm or at room temperature. It can be enjoyed on its own as a dessert or snack, or served alongside coffee or tea.

Tips:

- **Variations:** You can add a sprinkle of ground cinnamon or nutmeg to the batter for additional flavor. Some recipes also include a tablespoon of lime zest for a citrusy twist.
- **Storage:** Store leftover Pan de Elote in an airtight container at room temperature for up to 3 days. You can also freeze it for longer storage; thaw at room temperature before serving.
- **Fresh vs. Canned Corn:** If fresh corn isn't available, canned or frozen corn (thawed and drained) works well in this recipe. Just ensure to blend it until smooth.

Pan de Elote is a wonderful way to enjoy the natural sweetness of corn in a moist and flavorful cake. It's a perfect dessert or snack for any occasion, and its simplicity makes it a favorite among both kids and adults. Enjoy this traditional Mexican treat with friends and family!

Nopalitos Salad

Ingredients:

- 4-5 nopales (prickly pear cactus pads)
- 1 tomato, diced
- 1/2 small red onion, thinly sliced
- 1/4 cup chopped fresh cilantro
- 1 jalapeño or serrano chili, seeded and finely chopped (optional, for heat)
- 1 avocado, diced (optional, for added creaminess)
- 2 tablespoons olive oil
- 2 tablespoons fresh lime juice
- Salt and pepper, to taste

Instructions:

1. **Prepare the Nopales:**
   - Using tongs, hold each nopal pad over an open flame (gas stove) or grill, or in a hot dry skillet, to char the surface slightly. This step helps remove the slime and enhances the flavor.
   - Once charred, carefully scrape off any remaining spines using a knife. Rinse the nopales under cold water to remove any charred bits.
   - Slice the nopales into bite-sized pieces or strips.
2. **Assemble the Salad:**
   - In a large bowl, combine the sliced nopales, diced tomato, thinly sliced red onion, chopped cilantro, and finely chopped chili (if using).
   - If using avocado, gently fold in diced avocado to avoid mashing it.
3. **Dress the Salad:**
   - Drizzle olive oil and fresh lime juice over the salad ingredients.
   - Season with salt and pepper to taste.
4. **Mix and Chill:**
   - Toss the salad gently to combine all ingredients and coat them with the dressing evenly.
   - Refrigerate the Nopalitos Salad for at least 30 minutes to allow the flavors to meld together.
5. **Serve:**
   - Serve Nopalitos Salad chilled as a side dish or as a topping for tacos, tostadas, or grilled meats.

Tips:

- **Handling Nopales:** When preparing nopales, always wear gloves to protect your hands from the tiny spines. Char them briefly to remove the slime and improve texture.
- **Variations:** You can customize this salad by adding other ingredients like black beans, corn kernels, or diced bell peppers for additional flavor and texture.

- **Storage:** Nopalitos Salad can be stored in the refrigerator in an airtight container for up to 2 days. The flavors often improve as it sits, making it a great make-ahead dish for parties or gatherings.

Nopalitos Salad is a vibrant and healthy dish that celebrates the flavors of Mexico. It's a wonderful way to enjoy nopales, known for their unique texture and nutritional benefits. Try this refreshing salad for a taste of authentic Mexican cuisine!

Jericalla

Ingredients:

- 1 quart (4 cups) whole milk
- 1 cup granulated sugar
- 1 cinnamon stick (or 1/2 teaspoon ground cinnamon)
- 1 vanilla bean, split lengthwise (or 1 tablespoon vanilla extract)
- 6 large egg yolks
- 1/4 cup all-purpose flour
- Pinch of salt

Instructions:

1. **Prepare the Milk Mixture:**
   - In a saucepan, combine the whole milk, granulated sugar, cinnamon stick (or ground cinnamon), and the seeds scraped from the vanilla bean (or vanilla extract).
   - Heat the mixture over medium heat, stirring occasionally, until it comes to a simmer. Remove from heat and let it steep for about 10-15 minutes to infuse the flavors. If using a cinnamon stick and vanilla bean, remove them from the milk mixture after steeping.
2. **Prepare the Egg Mixture:**
   - In a large bowl, whisk together the egg yolks, all-purpose flour, and a pinch of salt until smooth and well combined.
3. **Combine and Cook:**
   - Gradually pour the warm milk mixture into the egg mixture, whisking constantly to temper the eggs. This step is crucial to prevent the eggs from curdling.
   - Once combined, pour the mixture back into the saucepan.
   - Cook over medium heat, stirring constantly with a wooden spoon or silicone spatula, until the mixture thickens and coats the back of the spoon. This should take about 8-10 minutes. Do not let it boil.
4. **Chill and Serve:**
   - Remove the saucepan from heat and pour the mixture through a fine mesh sieve into a bowl to remove any lumps.
   - Divide the mixture evenly among individual ramekins or custard cups.
   - Let the Jericalla cool to room temperature, then cover each ramekin with plastic wrap and refrigerate for at least 4 hours, or until set and chilled.
5. **Serve:**
   - Before serving, you can optionally sprinkle the tops with a thin layer of granulated sugar and use a kitchen torch to caramelize it, creating a crispy top layer similar to crème brûlée.
   - Alternatively, serve Jericalla chilled, garnished with a sprinkle of ground cinnamon or fresh berries.

Tips:

- **Vanilla Bean vs. Extract:** If using vanilla extract instead of a vanilla bean, add it after the mixture has been removed from heat, to preserve its flavor.
- **Texture:** Jericalla should have a smooth and creamy texture, similar to a custard. Make sure to stir constantly while cooking to avoid any lumps.
- **Storage:** Jericalla can be stored in the refrigerator for up to 3 days. Keep it covered to prevent it from absorbing other flavors.

Jericalla is a delightful dessert that combines the warmth of cinnamon and richness of vanilla with a creamy custard texture. It's a perfect way to end a Mexican-inspired meal or to enjoy on its own as a sweet treat.

Polvorones

Ingredients:

- 1 cup (2 sticks) unsalted butter, softened
- 1/2 cup powdered sugar, plus extra for coating
- 1 teaspoon vanilla extract
- 2 cups all-purpose flour
- 1 cup finely ground almonds or pecans (or a combination)
- 1/4 teaspoon salt

Instructions:

1. **Preheat and Prepare:**
   - Preheat your oven to 350°F (175°C). Line a baking sheet with parchment paper or silicone baking mat.
2. **Cream Butter and Sugar:**
   - In a large mixing bowl, cream together the softened butter and powdered sugar until light and fluffy.
3. **Add Vanilla and Dry Ingredients:**
   - Mix in the vanilla extract until well combined.
   - In a separate bowl, whisk together the flour, ground nuts, and salt.
4. **Combine Wet and Dry Ingredients:**
   - Gradually add the flour mixture to the butter mixture, mixing until the dough comes together and forms a soft dough. The dough should be slightly crumbly but hold together when pressed.
5. **Shape the Cookies:**
   - Scoop out portions of dough and roll them into small balls, about 1 inch in diameter, using your hands.
   - Place the balls on the prepared baking sheet, spacing them about 1 inch apart.
6. **Bake:**
   - Bake the cookies in the preheated oven for 12-15 minutes, or until the bottoms are lightly golden. The tops should remain pale.
7. **Cool and Coat:**
   - Remove the cookies from the oven and let them cool on the baking sheet for 5 minutes.
   - While still warm, gently roll each cookie in powdered sugar to coat them completely. Transfer the coated cookies to a wire rack to cool completely.
8. **Serve:**
   - Once cooled, dust the Polvorones with more powdered sugar if desired.
   - Store the cookies in an airtight container at room temperature. They will keep well for up to 1 week.

Tips:

- **Ground Nuts:** You can use almonds, pecans, or even walnuts for a different flavor. Make sure the nuts are finely ground to ensure a smooth texture in the cookies.
- **Variations:** Some recipes add a hint of cinnamon or a splash of almond extract for additional flavor. Feel free to experiment with different extracts or spices.
- **Handling:** Polvorones are delicate and crumbly, so handle them gently when rolling and coating with powdered sugar.

Polvorones are a delightful treat for any occasion, from weddings to holidays or simply for enjoying with a cup of coffee or tea. Their melt-in-your-mouth texture and nutty flavor make them a favorite in Mexican cuisine. Enjoy baking and sharing these delicious cookies with family and friends!

Huachinango a la Veracruzana

Ingredients:

- 4 red snapper fillets (about 6-8 ounces each), skin-on
- Salt and pepper, to taste
- All-purpose flour, for dusting (optional)
- 3 tablespoons olive oil
- 1 onion, thinly sliced
- 2 cloves garlic, minced
- 1 jalapeño or serrano chili, thinly sliced (optional, for heat)
- 1 red bell pepper, thinly sliced
- 1 can (14 ounces) diced tomatoes (preferably fire-roasted)
- 1/4 cup green olives, sliced
- 2 tablespoons capers, drained
- 1/2 teaspoon dried oregano
- 1/2 teaspoon dried thyme (or 1-2 sprigs fresh thyme)
- 1/2 teaspoon ground cumin
- 1/2 cup chicken or vegetable broth
- 1/4 cup fresh cilantro or parsley, chopped (for garnish)
- Lime wedges, for serving
- Cooked rice or warm tortillas, for serving

Instructions:

1. **Prepare the Red Snapper:**
   - Pat dry the red snapper fillets with paper towels. Season both sides with salt and pepper. Optionally, lightly dust the fillets with flour, shaking off any excess.
2. **Sear the Snapper:**
   - In a large skillet or frying pan, heat 2 tablespoons of olive oil over medium-high heat.
   - Place the snapper fillets in the skillet, skin-side down. Cook for about 3-4 minutes on each side, or until the skin is crispy and the fish flakes easily with a fork. Remove the snapper from the skillet and set aside.
3. **Make the Veracruzana Sauce:**
   - In the same skillet, add the remaining 1 tablespoon of olive oil if needed. Add the thinly sliced onion, minced garlic, and sliced chili (if using). Sauté for 2-3 minutes until the onions are softened and fragrant.
   - Add the sliced red bell pepper and continue to sauté for another 2-3 minutes, until the bell pepper begins to soften.
   - Stir in the diced tomatoes (with their juices), sliced green olives, drained capers, dried oregano, dried thyme (or fresh thyme sprigs), and ground cumin. Cook for 5-6 minutes, stirring occasionally, until the sauce has slightly thickened.
4. **Simmer the Fish in the Sauce:**

- Pour the chicken or vegetable broth into the skillet and bring the mixture to a simmer.
- Return the seared red snapper fillets to the skillet, nestling them into the sauce. Spoon some of the sauce over the fillets.
- Cover the skillet with a lid and let the fish simmer gently in the sauce for 5-7 minutes, or until the fish is cooked through and flakes easily.

5. **Serve:**
   - Garnish the Huachinango a la Veracruzana with chopped fresh cilantro or parsley.
   - Serve the red snapper fillets with the Veracruzana sauce spooned over the top. Accompany with lime wedges for squeezing over the fish.
   - Serve Huachinango a la Veracruzana hot, with cooked rice or warm tortillas on the side.

Tips:

- **Fish Selection:** If red snapper (huachinango) is not available, you can substitute it with other firm white fish fillets such as cod, halibut, or sea bass.
- **Spice Level:** Adjust the heat by adding more or less chili according to your preference. You can also leave out the chili for a milder dish.
- **Make-Ahead:** The Veracruzana sauce can be made ahead of time and refrigerated. Simply reheat it gently on the stove before adding the fish fillets.

Huachinango a la Veracruzana is a vibrant and flavorful dish that highlights the combination of tomatoes, olives, capers, and aromatic spices. It's a perfect choice for seafood lovers looking to explore authentic Mexican cuisine. Enjoy this dish as a main course for a special dinner or as part of a festive meal!

Esquites

Ingredients:

- 4 cups fresh corn kernels (about 4-5 ears of corn)
- 2 tablespoons butter or vegetable oil
- 1/4 cup mayonnaise
- 1/4 cup Mexican crema or sour cream
- 1/2 cup crumbled cotija cheese (or feta cheese)
- 1 teaspoon chili powder (adjust to taste)
- 1/2 teaspoon smoked paprika (optional)
- 1/4 cup chopped fresh cilantro
- 1 lime, cut into wedges
- Salt and pepper, to taste

Instructions:

1. **Prepare the Corn:**
   - If using fresh corn on the cob, remove the kernels from the cobs using a sharp knife. You should have about 4 cups of corn kernels.
2. **Cook the Corn:**
   - In a large skillet, heat the butter or vegetable oil over medium-high heat.
   - Add the corn kernels to the skillet and cook, stirring occasionally, for about 5-7 minutes, or until the corn is tender and lightly charred in spots. Adjust the heat as needed to prevent burning.
3. **Assemble Esquites:**
   - In a large bowl, combine the cooked corn kernels with the mayonnaise, Mexican crema or sour cream, and crumbled cotija cheese.
   - Season the mixture with chili powder, smoked paprika (if using), salt, and pepper. Stir well to combine.
4. **Serve:**
   - Divide the Esquites into serving bowls or cups.
   - Garnish each serving with chopped fresh cilantro and a squeeze of lime juice.
   - Serve immediately while warm, with extra lime wedges on the side for squeezing over the Esquites.

Tips:

- **Variations:** Esquites can be customized to your taste. You can add chopped green onions, diced jalapeños for heat, or even bacon bits for extra flavor.
- **Cheese Substitution:** If cotija cheese is not available, you can use crumbled feta cheese as a substitute.

- **Make-Ahead:** You can prepare the corn kernels ahead of time and assemble the Esquites just before serving. Keep the components separate and combine them when ready to serve.

Esquites are a delicious and comforting snack that captures the essence of Mexican street food. They are perfect for enjoying as a side dish, appetizer, or even a light meal. Serve them at your next gathering or enjoy them as a flavorful treat any time!

Alambre

Ingredients:

- 1 lb beef sirloin or skirt steak, thinly sliced
- 1 onion, thinly sliced
- 1 bell pepper (any color), thinly sliced
- 1-2 jalapeño peppers, thinly sliced (optional, for heat)
- 1 tomato, thinly sliced
- 8-10 slices of bacon, chopped into small pieces
- 1 tablespoon vegetable oil
- 1 tablespoon soy sauce
- 1 tablespoon Worcestershire sauce
- Salt and pepper, to taste
- 1 cup shredded Oaxaca cheese (or mozzarella cheese)
- Fresh cilantro, chopped, for garnish
- Lime wedges, for serving
- Warm tortillas, for serving

Instructions:

1. **Prepare the Meat:**
    - Heat a large skillet or frying pan over medium-high heat. Add the chopped bacon and cook until crispy. Remove the bacon from the pan and set aside, leaving the bacon fat in the pan.
    - Add the thinly sliced beef to the skillet in batches, ensuring not to overcrowd the pan. Cook the beef until browned and cooked through, about 2-3 minutes per batch. Remove the beef from the pan and set aside.
2. **Cook the Vegetables:**
    - In the same skillet, add the vegetable oil if needed. Add the sliced onion, bell pepper, jalapeño peppers (if using), and tomato slices. Sauté for 3-4 minutes until the vegetables are tender-crisp.
3. **Combine and Season:**
    - Return the cooked beef and bacon to the skillet with the vegetables. Add the soy sauce and Worcestershire sauce. Season with salt and pepper to taste. Stir well to combine and cook for another 2-3 minutes to heat everything through.
4. **Add Cheese and Serve:**
    - Sprinkle the shredded Oaxaca cheese (or mozzarella cheese) over the Alambre mixture in the skillet. Cover the skillet with a lid or aluminum foil and let it sit for a minute or two until the cheese is melted.
5. **Serve:**
    - Garnish the Alambre with chopped fresh cilantro.
    - Serve hot, with warm tortillas and lime wedges on the side.

Tips:

- **Meat Variation:** You can use other cuts of beef or pork for Alambre, such as flank steak, ribeye, or pork loin. Adjust cooking times accordingly based on the thickness of the meat.
- **Vegetables:** Feel free to customize the vegetables based on your preference. Mushrooms, zucchini, or even pineapple chunks can be added for extra flavor and texture.
- **Assembly:** Serve Alambre directly from the skillet for a rustic presentation, or transfer to a serving platter.

Alambre is a versatile and satisfying dish that's perfect for a casual dinner or a festive gathering. Enjoy wrapping the flavorful mixture in warm tortillas for a delicious Mexican meal!

Pescado Zarandeado

Ingredients:

- 1 whole red snapper (or other firm-fleshed fish), cleaned and butterflied
- For the Marinade:
    - 4 dried guajillo chilies, stemmed and seeded
    - 4 dried chiles de árbol, stemmed and seeded (adjust to taste for heat)
    - 3 cloves garlic, minced
    - 1/2 cup orange juice
    - 1/4 cup lime juice
    - 1/4 cup soy sauce
    - 1/4 cup Worcestershire sauce
    - 1/4 cup olive oil
    - 1 teaspoon ground cumin
    - 1 teaspoon dried oregano
    - Salt and pepper, to taste
- For Grilling:
    - Olive oil, for brushing
    - 1 lime, cut into wedges
- For Serving:
    - Fresh cilantro, chopped
    - Sliced red onion
    - Sliced avocado
    - Warm tortillas or rice

Instructions:

1. **Prepare the Marinade:**
    - In a bowl, soak the dried guajillo chilies and chiles de árbol in hot water for 15-20 minutes until softened. Drain the chilies.
    - In a blender or food processor, combine the softened chilies, minced garlic, orange juice, lime juice, soy sauce, Worcestershire sauce, olive oil, ground cumin, dried oregano, salt, and pepper. Blend until smooth to create the marinade.
2. **Marinate the Fish:**
    - Place the butterflied fish in a large dish or resealable plastic bag. Pour the marinade over the fish, making sure it is evenly coated. Cover the dish or seal the bag and refrigerate for at least 2 hours, or preferably overnight, to allow the flavors to penetrate the fish.
3. **Grill the Fish:**
    - Preheat the grill to medium-high heat. Brush the grill grates with olive oil to prevent sticking.

- Remove the fish from the marinade, shaking off any excess. Reserve the marinade for basting.
- Place the fish on the grill, skin-side down. Cook for about 5-7 minutes per side, depending on the thickness of the fish, basting occasionally with the reserved marinade. The fish is done when the flesh is opaque and flakes easily with a fork.

4. **Serve:**
   - Transfer the grilled fish to a serving platter. Garnish with chopped fresh cilantro and serve with sliced red onion, avocado slices, lime wedges, and warm tortillas or rice.

Tips:

- **Butterflying the Fish:** Butterflying the fish helps it cook more evenly on the grill and allows the marinade to penetrate deeper into the flesh.
- **Adjusting Heat:** You can adjust the amount of chiles de árbol used in the marinade to control the spiciness of the dish.
- **Variations:** Pescado Zarandeado is versatile. You can use different types of firm-fleshed fish such as snapper, sea bass, or grouper, depending on availability and preference.
- **Presentation:** Serve Pescado Zarandeado family-style on a large platter, allowing everyone to dig in and enjoy the flavorful fish with the accompaniments.

Pescado Zarandeado is a delicious and festive dish that celebrates the flavors of Mexico's coastal cuisine. It's perfect for gatherings or special occasions, bringing a taste of traditional Mexican grilling to your table.

Chile Ancho Rellenos

Ingredients:

- 6-8 dried ancho chiles
- 1 lb ground beef or pork (or a mixture)
- 1 onion, finely chopped
- 2 cloves garlic, minced
- 1 tomato, chopped
- 1/2 cup raisins
- 1/2 cup slivered almonds
- 1/2 cup chopped fresh cilantro
- 1/2 teaspoon ground cumin
- 1/2 teaspoon dried oregano
- Salt and pepper, to taste
- 1 cup chicken or vegetable broth
- 2 tablespoons vegetable oil, for frying

For the Batter:

- 4 eggs, separated
- 1/4 teaspoon salt
- 1/2 cup all-purpose flour

Instructions:

1. **Prepare the Ancho Chiles:**
   - Remove the stems from the ancho chiles and carefully slit them open lengthwise. Remove the seeds and veins, taking care not to tear the chiles. Rinse them under cold water and pat dry with paper towels.
2. **Prepare the Filling:**
   - In a skillet, heat the vegetable oil over medium heat. Add the chopped onion and minced garlic, sauté until softened and translucent, about 3-4 minutes.
   - Add the ground beef or pork to the skillet, breaking it up with a spoon. Cook until browned and cooked through, about 5-7 minutes.
   - Stir in the chopped tomato, raisins, slivered almonds, ground cumin, dried oregano, salt, and pepper. Cook for another 3-4 minutes, allowing the flavors to meld together.
   - Pour in the chicken or vegetable broth and simmer the mixture for 10-15 minutes, or until most of the liquid has evaporated and the filling is thickened. Remove from heat and stir in the chopped cilantro. Let the filling cool slightly.
3. **Stuff and Prepare the Chiles:**
   - Carefully stuff each prepared ancho chile with the filling mixture, ensuring they are evenly filled but not overstuffed.

4. **Make the Batter:**
    - In a large bowl, beat the egg whites with salt until stiff peaks form. In a separate bowl, lightly beat the egg yolks.
    - Gently fold the beaten egg yolks into the egg whites.
    - Spread the flour on a plate. Dip each stuffed ancho chile into the flour to coat lightly, then dip into the egg batter, making sure it is evenly coated.
5. **Fry the Chiles:**
    - In a large skillet or frying pan, heat about 1/2 inch of vegetable oil over medium-high heat until hot but not smoking.
    - Carefully place the battered chiles in the hot oil, a few at a time, and fry until golden brown and crispy on all sides, about 3-4 minutes per side. Use tongs to gently turn them.
    - Remove the fried chiles from the oil and place them on a plate lined with paper towels to drain excess oil.
6. **Serve:**
    - Serve the Chiles Anchos Rellenos hot, garnished with additional chopped cilantro if desired.
    - They can be served with Mexican rice, refried beans, salsa, or a side of fresh salad.

Tips:

- **Variations:** Instead of ground meat, you can use cheese such as Oaxaca cheese or panela cheese for a vegetarian version.
- **Baking Option:** If you prefer a healthier alternative, you can bake the stuffed chiles in the oven at 375°F (190°C) for 20-25 minutes, until the batter is golden brown and crispy.
- **Handling Chiles:** Handle the dried ancho chiles carefully to prevent tearing, as they can be fragile.

Chiles Anchos Rellenos are a wonderful representation of traditional Mexican cuisine, offering a delightful blend of flavors and textures. Enjoy making and savoring this delicious dish!

Tacos de Cabeza

Ingredients:

- 1 lb beef cabeza (beef cheeks), cleaned and trimmed of excess fat
- 1 onion, quartered
- 4 garlic cloves, peeled
- 2 bay leaves
- 1 teaspoon whole black peppercorns
- Salt, to taste
- Corn tortillas, warmed
- Chopped onion and cilantro, for garnish
- Salsa verde or salsa roja, for serving
- Lime wedges, for serving

Instructions:

1. **Prepare the Beef Cheeks:**
   - In a large pot or Dutch oven, combine the beef cabeza (beef cheeks) with enough water to cover them completely.
   - Add the quartered onion, garlic cloves, bay leaves, and whole black peppercorns to the pot.
   - Bring the water to a boil over medium-high heat, then reduce the heat to low. Cover and simmer gently for about 3-4 hours, or until the meat is very tender and easily shreds with a fork.
2. **Shred the Meat:**
   - Once the meat is tender, remove it from the pot and let it cool slightly. Reserve some of the cooking liquid.
   - Using two forks or your hands, shred the beef cabeza into bite-sized pieces. Season with salt to taste.
3. **Prepare the Tacos:**
   - Heat a skillet or griddle over medium-high heat. Warm the corn tortillas on both sides until they are soft and pliable.
   - To assemble the tacos, place a spoonful of the shredded beef cabeza onto each warm tortilla.
   - Top with chopped onion and cilantro.
4. **Serve:**
   - Serve the Tacos de Cabeza immediately, accompanied by salsa verde or salsa roja, and lime wedges on the side.

Tips:

- **Cooking Time:** Cooking the beef cabeza low and slow is key to achieving tender meat. You can also use a slow cooker for this process, cooking on low for 6-8 hours.

- **Flavor Variations:** Some recipes call for adding additional seasonings like cumin, Mexican oregano, or a splash of vinegar for added flavor depth.
- **Accompaniments:** Tacos de Cabeza are typically served with traditional toppings like chopped onion, cilantro, salsa, and lime wedges. You can also add radishes or pickled jalapeños for extra crunch and flavor.

Tacos de Cabeza are a delicious and authentic Mexican dish that showcases the flavors of slow-cooked beef cheeks. Enjoy these tacos as a savory and satisfying meal for any occasion!

Camotes Poblanos

Ingredients:

- 2-3 large sweet potatoes (camotes), peeled and cut into chunks
- 2 tablespoons vegetable oil or lard
- 1 onion, finely chopped
- 2 cloves garlic, minced
- 2 poblano peppers, roasted, peeled, seeded, and cut into strips
- 1 tomato, chopped
- 1 teaspoon dried oregano
- 1/2 teaspoon ground cumin
- Salt and pepper, to taste
- 1/2 cup chicken or vegetable broth
- Fresh cilantro, chopped, for garnish

Instructions:

1. **Prepare the Poblano Peppers:**
   - Roast the poblano peppers over an open flame or under the broiler until the skin is charred and blistered. Place them in a plastic bag or covered bowl for about 10 minutes to sweat, then peel off the charred skin, remove the seeds, and cut into strips.
2. **Cook the Sweet Potatoes:**
   - In a large skillet or frying pan, heat the vegetable oil or lard over medium heat. Add the chopped onion and minced garlic, sauté until softened and translucent, about 3-4 minutes.
   - Add the sweet potato chunks to the skillet and cook for 5-7 minutes, stirring occasionally, until they start to brown slightly.
3. **Combine Ingredients:**
   - Stir in the roasted poblano pepper strips, chopped tomato, dried oregano, ground cumin, salt, and pepper. Cook for another 2-3 minutes to allow the flavors to meld together.
4. **Simmer:**
   - Pour the chicken or vegetable broth into the skillet, reduce the heat to low, cover, and simmer for 15-20 minutes, or until the sweet potatoes are tender and cooked through. Stir occasionally and add more broth if needed to prevent sticking.
5. **Serve:**
   - Remove from heat and garnish with chopped fresh cilantro.
   - Serve the Camotes Poblanos hot as a side dish or as a vegetarian main dish. They can be enjoyed on their own or with warm tortillas.

Tips:

- **Variations:** You can add other ingredients such as corn kernels, diced bell peppers, or a pinch of smoked paprika for additional flavor.
- **Spice Level:** Adjust the spiciness by adding or reducing the amount of poblano peppers used.
- **Make-Ahead:** Camotes Poblanos can be prepared ahead of time and reheated gently on the stove before serving. The flavors often meld together even more when reheated.

Camotes Poblanos are a comforting and flavorful dish that highlights the sweet and savory combination of sweet potatoes with roasted poblanos. Enjoy this traditional Mexican recipe as part of a hearty meal!

www.ingramcontent.com/pod-product-compliance
Lightning Source LLC
LaVergne TN
LVHW081601060526
838201LV00054B/2008